THE ULTIMATE FINANCIAL FREEDOM FRAMEWORK

THE ULTIMATE FINANCIAL FREEDOM FRAMEWORK

A Complete Guide to Achieving
Financial Independence

Pawan KR Agarwal

JAICO PUBLISHING HOUSE

Ahmedabad Bangalore Chennai
Delhi Hyderabad Kolkata Mumbai

Published by Jaico Publishing House
A-2 Jash Chambers, 7-A Sir Phirozshah Mehta Road
Fort, Mumbai - 400 001
jaicopub@jaicobooks.com
www.jaicobooks.com

THE ULTIMATE FINANCIAL FREEDOM FRAMEWORK
ISBN 978-93-49358-30-0

First Jaico Impression: 2025

Page design and layout by Jojy Philip, Delhi

Printed by
Parksons Graphics Pvt. Ltd., Mumbai

To,

Goddess Lakshmi

CONTENT

ACKNOWLEDGMENTS

I want to extend my sincere gratitude to everyone who has helped make writing and publishing this book possible. I am grateful to the editorial team at Jaico Publishing House for their assistance, encouragement, and help in giving this book a form and structure.

I would like to thank my good friend Asit Pandya for proofreading and editing my book and supporting me as I wrote it. I express my sincere thanks and gratitude to CA Vimal Punmiya, CA Shashikant Maiya, and Harshad Chetanwala for contributing chapters on estate planning, tax planning, and stocks and mutual funds respectively in this book.

I appreciate the tireless efforts of my employees, Neeta, Preethi, and Prashant in finishing the assignment; major part of this manuscript has been typed by Neeta herself. The manuscript was thoroughly reviewed by my daughter-in-law, Prerna, who made numerous valuable suggestions that were promptly included. I want to thank my wife Pushpa, my sons Piyush and Ankur, my elder daughter-in-law Krati, and all my family members for their tolerance and patience. I would also like to thank my grandchildren Dhruv and Dhwani for their excitement and energy.

I want to publicly thank my mentors Jay Kabir, Amit Pathak, and Partha Gupta for supporting, directing, and teaching me throughout my life.

This book includes numerous examples, tales, and anecdotes from newspapers, periodicals, and various biographies I have come across over the years, as well as insights gained from the several seminars I have hosted over the past 20 years. Unfortunately, it's not possible to cite exact sources as some aren't available thereby making it impractical to precisely acknowledge them. However, I still would like to thank everyone who might have helped with this work, whether anonymously or otherwise, regardless of the source. My apologies for any omissions in giving credit wherever necessary. Corrections may be incorporated into future editions, if brought to my attention.

Finally, I want to express my gratitude to all my beloved readers for having faith in me and reading this book. I hope I can make the time that you spend reading this book worthwhile. I am on a mission to help one million individuals change their lives so that they may become financially independent and effortless leaders. You may connect with me at lionpawankr@gmail.com, or, visit my website www. indiagrowthacademy.com.

I sincerely hope you enjoy reading this book as much as I enjoyed writing it.

I love you.

—**Pawan KR Agarwal**

CHAPTER 1

INTRODUCTION

"A great deed is rarely done at the first attempt."
—Napoleon Bonaparte, French military general and statesman

At some point in your early life, you might have come across the following short and witty poem:

> *Money, money, come to me*
> *Come, come, come today*
> *I need you in plenty,*
> *Come! come! come!*

Who does not want to create wealth and lead a life free of financial worries? Yet, achieving financial freedom cannot be your ultimate goal. It is just an energy junction in the journey towards living the life you wish to live. You must have a concrete agenda to pursue financial freedom. Attaining financial freedom is not a sprint; it's a marathon. So, be ready to remain motivated during this lifelong journey.

WHAT IS FINANCIAL FREEDOM?

Financial freedom is broadly defined as having enough financial resources to pay for your living expenses, in addition to achieving many of your life goals without having to work extra or otherwise commit any of your time or efforts to generating money.

Freedom can mean different things to different people. To some, it may mean doing what they love the most or being free from financial responsibilities. To others, it may mean enjoying life without worrying about income. And to some, it may mean devoting their time to society's welfare by contributing to the needs of the less fortunate or protecting the environment.

Do you think wealth should be understood only in terms of money?

Author Megha Bajaj explores different aspects of freedom in her article—'*Five Faces of Freedom*'.[1] She shares the following connotations of freedom:

1) Freedom of health

2) Financial freedom

3) Freedom to do what you love

4) Freedom in relationships

5) Spiritual freedom

Financial freedom, without the freedom in other areas of our lives, holds no meaning.

Further into this book, we will explore the possibilities of achieving financial goals, which are realistic and practical. Many legends have amassed enormous wealth and become billionaires. But the fact remains that only some—say one in a million—are able to achieve this feat. So, a pragmatic and prudent approach should be to focus on setting achievable goals.

Being financially free does not mean you have to only be a millionaire or a billionaire; even a wage earner drawing an amount of ₹25,000 a month has an equal right to be financially free. If that same wage earner saves a minimum of ₹5,000 per month and tops it up by 5% every year, they can accumulate a corpus of ₹8 crores in 35 years. To be financially free, you don't need to save a huge amount every month, nor is it required to earn a fantastic return rate.

Let me list down a few perks of being financially free:

1. You are free from all financial burdens.

2. You feel relaxed and are free to pursue your passion or hobbies. Today, I am financially free, and my passion is to guide others to follow suit. I have already written my first book—*12 Mantras of Effortless Leadership*—a couple of years ago, and this is my second non-technical book. I have almost finished writing my third book as well. I could not have pursued my passion for writing books had I struggled to earn my active income. I see endless possibilities now to be creative. Your passion might generate extra income with little effort.

3. You can take calculated risks as you already have a large corpus.

4. You can contribute to society in the areas of your liking. For example, providing holistic support to the youth, contributing towards humanitarian needs such as eradicating hunger, protecting environment, assisting the differently abled, spreading awareness about diabetes and other diseases, and so on.

But to reach to this stage of financial freedom, you need to keep in mind following prerequisites:

1. Earn a steady, passive income from investments.

2. Make appropriate provisions for specific events like marriages, vacations, education, etc.

3. Be prepared for any unforeseen expenses in the future such as medical emergencies, urgent home repairs, etc.

4. Deploy your time and energy creatively.

5. Be inclined to serve the community.

6. Pursue your passion, hobbies, and things you love to do.

7. Maintain emotional stability in relationships.

8. Ensure that inherited money is not frittered away through hyper-consumerist behaviour.

9. Respect money at every stage of your life; whether you are struggling to earn or manage money or when you are filthy rich.

Money is earned, but wealth is created. You must endeavour to creating wealth even as you are earning. So, *what is the number you think will look good in your bank account?* That is entirely subjective. Generally, this is the corpus you will need to meet all your expenses when you retire—forced or planned.

This number should be at least 20 times your current annual expenses. If your annual expenses are ₹10 lakhs, you need at least ₹2 crores worth investments in your asset portfolio at the time of retirement. You may ask why 20 and not 10 times. The answer is simple: your expenses will at least double or triple after 15 or 20 years because of inflation. Presuming the inflation rate at 6%, your expenses will double in 12 years and, naturally, quadruple in 24 years. Let's discuss in depth how to achieve this goal.

Awareness is the first step to achieving financial freedom. Planning and action come later on. You wish to be financially free because you want more free time to do the things you want to do, not what you need to do. At the same time, you want to contribute to society in your own ways.

True financial freedom is doing what you love to do. Then, it does not matter when you retire. You may work until you are over 80 years old, provided your work is your passion, it motivates you daily, and gives you a reason to wake up early in the morning.

So, what exactly is financial freedom? Financial freedom is when your passive income exceeds your current expenses and manages to beat inflation. Passive income means you do not work for money; money works for you. However, financial freedom is not only about money; it has more to do with feelings, because, as you already know, money does not always bring happiness.

THE WHEEL OF LIFE

Finance is not everything; there are many aspects of life besides finance. I have seen several people whose lives are unbalanced. Many among them need to familiarize themselves with the concept: *the wheel of life*. Some are so intoxicated by ambition and greed that they only aspire to achieve name, fame, and wealth, thereby ignoring all the other areas of life. There are nine areas of your life that need your equal attention—health, relationships, learning, career, recreation, prosperity, extended family and friends, spirituality, and contribution to society. You must take appropriate action to balance each area of your life.

The *wheel of life*, also known as the *life balance wheel*, helps you determine which parts of your life need more energy and time to balance. Many graphical tools are available online, and you can use them to your benefit. The principle is simple—you must make it a habit. In my experience, as little as five minutes of daily practice is enough to master the concept of the wheel of life.

Major hurdles in executing any action are lack of challenging goal(s), no *why* (well-defined purpose), and a habit of procrastination. Setting inspirational goals keeps you motivated and gives you a sense of direction. You become accountable and can then create milestones and measure your progress.

In 2008 Beijing Olympics, Michael Phelps—American swimmer and one of the most celebrated Olympians of all time with 28 medals— had won most gold medals (eight) in every event he entered that year and set new world records. To learn a few of his success secrets would be fantastic.

Revealing how he managed to stay focussed and motivated throughout his wins, Michael once said in an interview, "I didn't look at the sheet (goal sheet) every day. I pretty much memorized it, how fast I wanted to swim, and what I had to do to get there. If there were a day when I was down, not swimming well, or simply feeling tired or grouchy, I would look at it. It worked as a pick-me-up."

His coach, Bob Bowman, always said, *"Can't* and *won't* carry different implications. You limit what you can or will do if you say you *can't*, but *won't* gives you a choice." Bob emphasized that the most important factor in anything we do, particularly in this endeavour of staying motivated, is our daily attitude. His slogan was, *"Attitude, Action, Achievement.* That's the order in which you could expect things to happen. You could either see every day's practice as an ordeal, or, you could see it as an adventure. We become what we think about the most. You will be an Olympic champion in attitude long before there's a gold medal around your neck."[2]

"When we practice long and hard, Bob would say we are depositing money into the bank. We need to deposit enough so that when we make a large withdrawal, and we have enough funds to do so," Michael added.

The journey towards financial freedom is no different. You have to step out of your comfort zone; learn to be comfortable even in an uncomfortable situation. That is how you gradually move out of your comfort zone and eventually break free from its golden prison. It is only then you start giving your 100 percent. You put your soul into whatever you do. You use your heart as well as your intellect. Sunil Saxena—author of *Massive Action Equals Massive Results*—nicely explains this concept: "If you are taking massive action with a *go big or go home* mentality, you might undertake those things that move you toward your desired high-level success. If you have a wait-and-see approach, you might try one thing at a time and never achieve success.[3]

Sushil Mehta of Jains Car Shoppe (Chennai)—who, from a modest beginning, became the CEO of an enterprise run by 700 employees— proudly says, for him, sincerity means, "Giving my 111% to anything I take up. Either I do not take up a responsibility, or if I do, I will give it every breath that I have."[4] This, in my opinion, is a perfect example of *massive action.*

Grant Cardone is known for his massive real estate empire. He is also a sales coach, best-selling author, and motivational speaker. In

The 10X Rule, he says, "When I embark on a project, whether it is writing a new book, creating a seminar program, developing a new product, starting a new workout, improving my marriage, or spending time with my daughter, I go at it completely. I'm all in, fully committed, like a hungry dog on the back of a meat truck."[5]

The story of Chairman and Managing Director of Nyati Group, Nitin Nyati—someone who believes in persistently taking on challenges—is equally inspiring. Good things seemed to be gracing Nitin from all directions. His every adventure made him realize how important it was to listen to the *call of the soul*. Had he chosen the comfort zone over taking over a fresh adventure, he would have never grown the way he did. He always asked himself a question, which became his life's mantra—"When was the last time you did something for the first time?" "Life," he realized, "belongs to those who are ready to take the plunge into the unknown."[6]

Financial freedom is the natural outcome of money management. But many of us do not know how to make, manage, invest, grow, enjoy, multiply money, and live a debt-free life. Our educational curriculum never tells us this. On the contrary, we are conditioned to the negative aspects of money.

GO BACK TO BASICS!

It is my firm belief that to become financially free, one has to follow the basics, which are as simple as crossing the road. You must:

a) Learn the basics of saving, spending, and investing

b) Execute the basics

c) Stick to the basics

I have realized that despite living in the age of information overload and easy access to coaching, training, and excellent lectures on financial planning, basics never change. *Cambridge Dictionary* defines the word 'basic' as "simple and not complicated, so able to provide the base or starting point from which something can develop." Basics are fundamental to help understand, apply, learn, integrate, or assimilate any skill, subject, or learning. They are the timeless cardinal principles one must know in order to build superstructures.

Everything that I discuss in this book is quite simple. However, just go back to the basics if you find it complicated, confusing, or contradictory. Understanding the basics may seem simple on the surface, however, it may get challenging as we dig deeper.

Stressing on the importance of acing the fundamentals of a game, American football coach and executive in the National Football League (NFL), Vince Lombardi, once said: "Games are decided by the basics." The same applies to football, cricket, any other game or aspect of your life for that matter. You may learn advanced techniques to ace any activity you undertake, but always remember the basics. So, the next time, try focusing on the basics instead of searching for a difficult answer to a problem. Reviewing your basics would make your foundation strong.

At the same time, note that there is no chartered path in the journey towards achieving financial freedom. There are no set directions. Each individual has to take their own path. In my career of over three decades, I have personally seen many rags-to-riches stories as well as the opposite. If you are from Mumbai, you may have noticed that an extremely rich person, in a turn of events, becomes broke and is compelled to sell his or her spacious house located at, say, an affluent suburb in South Mumbai like Walkeshwar and buy a modest house somewhere in a far-flung suburb like Nalasopara. Similarly, sometimes fortune may favour someone so much that a person living in Nalasopara affords to move to an affluent locality in South Mumbai. A residential house might cost between ₹15 and ₹20 crores in Walkeshwar. However, you may purchase a similar house in Nalasopara at less than ₹50 lakhs or so.

LESSONS FROM COVID-19 PANDEMIC

The COVID-19 pandemic created a grim situation that exposed us to new and unforeseen challenges. While many felt disconnected from the world due to mandatory isolation, many lost their jobs or had to manage their household expenses on half or no salary and for several months in a row. On the bright side, it taught us new critical lessons. Most of us began to manage this crisis with financial planning and perseverance. And those who had were frugal enough and had savings and emergency reserves faced fewer problems.

As a financial coach, when I ask people to save up to 20% of their income, they give excuses of rising costs, inflation, and lack of money. If they could survive on 50% of their income during a pandemic, why can't they survive by spending 80% of their income now? The pandemic brought in a new sense of frugality and financial discipline. We need to continue to inculcate this mindset for a better future.

MINDSET

Though it's true that frugality, saving, investments, etc., play a vital role in amassing wealth, at the end of the day, you must earn, increase your income, and have multiple sources of income. No one can teach you about money like physics (with rules and laws). It has to be taught like psychology (with emotions and nuance), as Morgan Housel aptly puts it in *The Psychology of Money*: "It's a mindset that determines your financial future rather than the simple math of compounding and saving."

A poor mindset cannot create a rich person. Everything in this world happens twice: first in our minds and then in the outer world. Suppose one believes wealth creation is immoral or can be created only by manipulating things, then they must change this negative thinking to an affirmative one. Wealth creation is not ostensibly a sign of immorality neither is it always achieved through unfair means. One should rather believe that they can make good use of wealth to help society by contributing towards education, medical relief, and protection of environment. There are divine and respectable ways of creating wealth, too, and one must be proud of it. Most wealthy people are great philanthropists, so one must respect them rather than judge them for their wealth.

ATTITUDE

All said and done, sometimes you have to face the music even if you do not like the tune. In case of a breakdown, you cannot blame others. You have to take responsibility for everything that happens to you and ensure that you are taking charge of your financial life. When something does not go as planned or falls short of one's expectations, or when there is a breakdown, instead of blaming others or circumstances, a good leader introspects and tries to find out whether the problem lies with the organizational structure or team dynamics or the processes that the organization is following. Remember that your success ultimately depends on your persistent will to improve, change, and innovate.

As per my experience (and that of many others), the happiest people do not blame others for their circumstances; they take responsibility. Long ago, in a seminar, when I asked the audience, "How many of you feel that you are solely responsible for your problems," only a few hands went up. However, when I asked, "How many of you feel that others or circumstances are responsible for your problems?", a large majority of the audience agreed with a show of hands. Some preferred being neutral and didn't raise their hands.

Many use 'blame' as a handy defense mechanism to avoid confronting the root cause of the problem, challenge, or issue. At times, they blame others despite knowing quite well that they themselves are at fault. This is because it's easier than owning responsibility; being accountable for your actions requires more energy than blaming others.

You must realize that everything exists in your life as your own creation. This realization completely dissolves the blame game. So, take the responsibility for where your life was, where it is heading at present, and where you hope it shall be. There is great freedom in this realization. Some obstacles are inevitable. Sometimes you win, and sometimes you don't. Just keep one crucial thing in mind that blaming others diminishes your power. You foster feelings of helplessness and pessimism. So, take ownership and learn from every experience. You are the cause and solution to all your problems. Nobody is perfect in this world.

So, be ready to take responsibility, stop the blame game, create your own reality, and know that—

- Financial freedom is your birthright
- You alone are responsible for your financial future
- Financial independence is possible no matter the circumstances you may be in

Take a solemn oath to take complete responsibility to make yourself financially free, come what may.

My mentor used to say that magic begins when logic ends. From the bottom of my heart, I advise that you raise your right hand and repeat the following affirmation, preferably before a mirror. Do it now.

> *"From this moment on, I take complete responsibility of becoming financially free and making today the most important, prominent, prosperous, and positive day of my life."*

CHAPTER 2

MINDSET

"Believe you can and you're halfway there."
—Theodore Roosevelt, 26th president of the United States

Being wealthy and financially free is a game of mind—entirely dependent on your mindset. In any case, your mindset plays a vital role in determining results in every area of your life. What you believe largely impacts your success. It's, therefore, essential to have a positive and strong mindset that helps you focus on your intentions. Jesus once said, "To those who believe, all things are possible."

You need to set your mind, body, and soul on what you want. A rich mindset reflects on everything you do. Same is with poor mindset. Unless you work on your mindset, you won't be able to achieve steady success. You need not follow everything mentioned in this chapter. For some, this chapter may appear a bit lengthy. However, before you dismiss any ideas presented here, do give it a good thought. American financial advisor and author Suze Orman aptly says, "We all have a wisdom within us that will tell us, if we listen to it, how to act with our money and with every other aspect of our lives. To get in touch with that voice from the core of our being is not only a step toward financial freedom, it's also a step toward spiritual serenity."[7]

Let's understand the entire gamut of mindset through the following aspects:

1. Having a rich mindset

2. Average mindset vs. rich mindset

3. Taking responsibility

4. Having a purpose

5. Living fearlessly

6. Law of attraction

7. Kubera mudra

8. Maintaining your piggy bank

9. Respecting money

10. Dreaming, planning, and taking action

11. Affirmations

1. HAVING A RICH MINDSET

It's a no-brainer that everybody needs money; you cannot survive without it. But your values, beliefs, and purpose determine the level of money you earn. You cannot become rich with a mind that operates on a poor blueprint. You should strive to have a wealthy mindset. For that, you need to start thinking of being rich first. You must respect, value, and love money. Be aware that to be rich is your birthright. Nature has abundant resources to support the humankind; it wants all of us to live in abundance.

Sushil Kumar, the first contestant to win ₹5 crores in the fifth season of the popular quiz show *Kaun Banega Crorepati*, soon became bankrupt after he hit the jackpot. This is because he was not mentally prepared to handle the windfall. He continued to be the person with the same mindset he had before this unexpected turn of events. He perhaps lacked awareness on how to deal with his sudden wealth, let alone grow and multiply it. Many lottery winners, especially the ones hailing from humble backgrounds, lose all their money within a few months of their win. It is simply because their mindset continues to operate on a poor blueprint. Nobody taught them money management.

We know of many film stars and celebrities who live in a debilitating financial situation towards the end of their careers. Former Indian cricketer Vinod Kambli, whose achievements have always been appreciated by one and all, was never seen without his gold chains, bracelets, and an expensive watch on his person. Today, he struggles to live a reasonably decent life on the professional front. Financially, he is in a mess. I wish he could have learned these mantras of financial freedom when he was in his 20s and 30s.

I would like to impress on the point that if you want to become rich, you must first work on your mind. Lord Buddha says we become what we think. Change your thought process. Chirag Aggarwal, the managing partner of Kokos Natural, says that if you give ₹10,000 to a rich person, he will return ₹10,000. But if you provide the same amount to a poor person, he will probably buy a mobile phone. Remember, the universe will never give you more than you can manage. If you cannot handle ₹1 lakh today, it is certain that you will not be able to handle ₹1 crore tomorrow. Respect whatever you have, manage it properly, and follow the rules of the money game.

Throughout my book I have been advocating to save and invest at least 10% or more from your regular income. During an interaction with one of my clients, a staff asked me how can he save and invest when his total monthly income is a meagre ₹15,000? In a city like Mumbai, it is difficult to manage a family of four persons in ₹15,000 per month. I advised that it is the mindset which is important, not the quantum of money he saves. Probably he can work little harder, pursue a part-time job on weekends or find a new source of income and earn say ₹500 to ₹1,000 extra per month. I can bet, that if he approaches his employer and requests him to increase his salary by ₹500 or so, he will get a positive answer. (Many employees I know have tried it successfully.) This extra income can be saved and invested. It does not matter whether you save 5% or 10% or even more. It's the habit which is important. If you can't save now, you will not save when your income is ₹25,000 or ₹30,000 or more.

True financial freedom simply means you don't have to work full-time post your retirement (age is irrelevant). You reach that stage in your life where you have the luxury to not work because you have to. You are able to pursue a passion close to your heart. You plan beyond financial security and consider aspects like spirituality, physical and emotional health, contribution to society, recreation, pursuing your hobbies and excitement. It simply means your experience lies in its totality. English writer Samuel Johnson once rightly said, "It's better to live rich than to die rich."

A rich mindset does not mean that you be extravagant and spend liberally. A rich person follows most of the mantras of financial freedom. They largely follow the simple formula—spend reasonably, earn more, and invest wisely. They know that growth brings security. They increase the size of their cake. For example, if your income is ₹5 lakhs per annum and you spend 10% on vacations, holidays, and recreation, you will be spending ₹50,000 only. But if you increase your income to ₹20 lakhs by spending the same percentage of 10%, you can plan to spend ₹2,00,000. So, raise your income by developing the requisite skills, having multiple sources of income, and ensuring passive income, such as dividends, royalty, interests, rent, capital gains, retainership fees, freelancing, subcontracting, etc.

T. Harv Eker, author of the best-selling book *Secrets of the Millionaire Mind,* says, "When self-made millionaires lose their money, they usually have it back within a relatively short time. Donald Trump is a good example. He was worth billions, lost everything, and then a couple of years later, got it all back again and more."[8] He lost his wealth, not his rich mindset. Remember, your outer world is the truest reflection of your inner world—your mindset.

2. AVERAGE MINDSET VS. RICH MINDSET

People with an average mindset are always in survival mode. They prefer to remain in their comfort zone and are not ambitious enough to create a future they want. The root cause of the same is the conditioning and environment in which they are brought up that eventually shapes their poor mindset over time.

On the other hand, people with a growth-oriented and rich mindset break free from the golden prison of their comfort zone. They cultivate the habit of positive thinking, discipline, saving, and investing, budget planning, etc.

The following table will tell you the difference between an average and a rich mindset:

AVERAGE MINDSET	RICH MINDSET
They blame others for their miseries.	They take responsibility and are proactive.
They wait for good things to manifest in their life.	They set their goals, make a plan, and take action to make things happen.
They chase pleasure and comfort.	They chase purpose.
They spend most of their time gossiping with friends or doomscrolling online. They waste time.	They make the best use of their time by surrounding themselves with successful people, and those with a growth mindset. They invest their time in productive pursuits.
They spend money on branded products.	They spend money on learning, inspiring books, skills, etc.
They buy luxury items on credit cards.	They buy only when they can afford it.
They think becoming rich is not their cup of tea.	For them, to be rich is their birthright.
"It is difficult to become rich—I am unlucky. I do not know how to become rich."	"I am a powerful money magnet. There are ethical ways of becoming rich and I am aware of them."
They learn from their own mistakes.	They learn from others' mistakes.
They are income-driven; their focus is on paycheck.	They are growth- and goal-driven, and believe in expansion.
They can hardly afford to do any charity.	They always have a budget for charity.

AVERAGE MINDSET	RICH MINDSET
They spend everything they earn.	They invest first and spend later.
They have only one source of income.	They have multiple sources of income.
They need money to make more money.	They need a growth mindset and skills to make money.
They do not know their net worth and financial goal.	They regularly track their net worth and review the same at least every six months.
They dress to impress others.	They dress to impress themselves and feel good.
They buy liabilities.	They buy assets.
They enjoy weekends.	They work hard to develop new skills and earn extra on weekends.
They believe in immediate gratification.	They believe in delayed gratification.
They do not take risks.	They take calculated risks.
They depend on good luck and wait for opportunities.	They depend on preparation. They know that luck is the meeting point of preparation and opportunity.
When they face difficulties, they lower their goals.	They upgrade themselves and raise their bar.
They envy their competitors.	They appreciate their competitors.
They see scarcity everywhere.	They see abundance everywhere.

AVERAGE MINDSET	RICH MINDSET
They have marginal growth every year.	They have quantum growth year after year.
They have no plans to create a great life.	They have a concrete plan to design a life they dream of.
They do not use the power of mind.	They know the power of subconscious mind.

The million-dollar question is whether you can change a mindset from an average one to a rich one. Can we reset the brain? The answer is yes. First, you have to identify your limiting beliefs and then replace them with empowering and goal-driven ones.

The affirmations given at the end of this chapter might help you. At the cost of repetition, I must say that unless you change the internal world, your outer and your physical world will not change. Work on your purpose and identity, and your values will change your environment and behaviour. If your identity resonates with "I am financially free", you will automatically behave accordingly, such as finding a new source of income, saving, investing, etc. Your environment will start supporting you.

So, start working on yourself at the earliest. If you have lot of chronic limiting beliefs, I suggest you take help of a licensed Neuro-Linguistic Programming (NLP) practitioner (or any other similar therapists) as these beliefs cannot be developed only by reading books.

In my advanced seminars, I coach people to get rid of limiting beliefs. For details, visit www.indiagrowthacademy.com.

3. TAKING RESPONSIBILITY

Taking full responsibility of your financial well-being is a mandatory step in the journey of becoming financially free. Our scriptures repeatedly assert that everything exists in one's life as its own creations. Taking responsibility completely dissolves the blame game. Take responsibility for where your life was, where it is now, and where it shall be; there is great freedom in this realization.

According to Brian Tracy, a well-known motivational speaker and self-development author who has authored over 80 books, "All negative emotions, especially anger, depend on your ability to blame someone or something else for something in your life that you are unhappy about."

Titus Peevy, in his excellent book *Blame Yourself! How to Take Responsibility and Improve Yourself in a Balanced Manner*, categorically mentions: "If you want to turn your life around, if you want to become the best you can be, you have to take responsibility and take the blame for your current situation. Responsibility for yourself and your life situation is the foundation on which you improve yourself, which is the most important thing anyone could ever do."

This book will show you the way and probably inspire you, but it's *you* who have to take action. A right mindset coupled with action will take you to your desired destination of financial freedom.

Remember that you alone are responsible for your financial well-being. Nobody else can do this for you. I suggest that you raise your right hand and repeat the following affirmation once again:

"From this moment on I take complete responsibility of becoming financially free, and making today the most important, prominent, prosperous and positive day of my life."

4. HAVING A PURPOSE

We have seen one can't become rich unless one is operating from a rich mindset. No one has become rich by operating from a poor mental blue print. We are what we think. In Neuro-linguistic Programming (NLP), there is a powerful tool called Neurological Levels Model, which consists of organizing our thinking, information gathering, communication, belief system, behaviour, and environment. Simply speaking, it starts with our mission which serves as a guiding light in our journey of life. Once we have clarity of our mission, we create our identity and belief system. In other words, we find our purpose, our *why*. Then we acquire the requisite skills, modify our behaviour, and influence the environment. This way, we work internally as well as externally. Unless the internal world is purposeful and self-serving, the external world will not support us. A mindset is nothing but creating a balance between our internal and our external worlds.

I suggest you ask the following questions to yourself:

- Why should the universe make me prosperous?
- Why should riches enter my life?
- Am I willing to pay the price for prosperity?
- Do I know that nature or the universe never gives, it returns?

- How will my prosperity help in making this world a better place to live?
- What is my *mission* in life?
- What is my *why*?
- What is my vision?

A purpose-centered life is the one where you can find your depth. Your purpose is your *mission*. It's your final goal. It's your *why*. It motivates you, day in and day out. It provides clarity in your life. Once you have clarity on your purpose, you become unstoppable and deeply committed to pursue your final goals. Eventually, your passion to pursue your purpose drives you. There is no need to waste your time on ordinary goals; focus on major ones. You then tend to face setbacks, if any, head-on, and bounce back quickly with double the force. This also makes you throw away your mask and become your true self.

So, it is important to know your purpose, your values, your mission, or your baseline. This is what we call life's purpose; if you ask me to put it concisely, I'd say: "Find something you love, work at it, and enjoy it."

Your *why* in your life is like the guiding light which keeps you on track in your journey of leadership.

For instance, take a look at this mission statement of *Diabetes Health*—a bi-monthly journal on diabetes. You will see the clarity in their purpose.

- To spread awareness and knowledge of diabetes and its consequences throughout India.

- To motivate the population to take preventive measures.

- To empower all those affected to participate in their own healthcare management.

I would like quote my own purpose in life:

> *"To develop friendship, faith, and optimism in life, as well as demonstrate leadership by contributing to society and making others prosperous."*

When Jamsetji Tata, founder of the Tata Group, built the iconic The Taj Mahal Palace, his sole wish was to attract foreigners to India. It was his love for Bombay (now Mumbai) and India that drove him to build this hotel. He believed that the building a luxury hotel in Mumbai could be seen as one of the essential signs of the city's progress.

Since this hotel was built in 1903, it has been known as India's finest luxury hotel and continues to epitomize the spirit of Mumbai and India. For Jamsetji, the *why* was so powerful that it urged him to stake his reputation, withstand all skepticism, and spend huge amount of resources to create the iconic hotel.

When the *why* is powerful enough, the *what* and *how* eventually reveal themselves to us and are fulfilled in many ways, particularly because we live life once, figuring out our own *why* is so important to unlocking the power of our lives.[9]

So, what is your *why*?

One way of finding your *why* is to answer the question: "What else would you love to do, if the money was not the concern?"

Most people are motivated by money; it may not be their prime driver but it definitely serves as a catalyst. So, look at your current job position or profession and ask yourself if you would still be doing it if you weren't concerned about money. If not, what would you do? Make sure to keep your aspirations realistic because, odds are, not all of you would end up as a runway model or a professional athlete. Think deeply for a moment about the kind of life you envision for yourself. If what you are presently doing doesn't fit into this category, you would just end up being stuck in a job you may never like. In reality, you should look for a career in a field which will make you happy, and keep you motivated to head to work every day with all your heart.[10]

So, go out and find your *why*!

There are certain rituals or set processes to attract wealth and become prosperous. You will get to know them as you read ahead.

5. LIVING FEARLESSLY

One of my clients shared an interesting story of his childhood. Once he stole some money from his father's waistcoat pocket and bought some balloons. His plan was to sell the balloons at a high price so that he could earn double the money and return the exact amount he stole to his father. Unfortunately, not a single the balloon got sold and soon most of them even burst. He lost the balloons as well as the money. He experienced his first failure in life. The client's father, however, had hardly noticed this theft as his son had stolen only a few coins from his waistcoat pocket. But this incident instilled a deep guilt, fear of failure, and a pattern of inaction in my client. This later on had an adverse impact on all his life's decisions.

As an adult, he never ventured out of his comfort zone and stuck with the same job even though several good opportunities knocked at his door. Even in his current job, when his employer offered him a small partnership, he refused out of fear of not succeeding at it. Because of his decisions, his life turned into a nightmare of losses, inaction, despondency, and bad luck.

As a financial adviser, it was crucial for me to understand the cause of my client's deep-rooted fear and feeling of guilt.

The truth is, the more you are afraid to face your challenges, the stronger this fear sets in your mind. However, if you face it head on, it will disappear. Spiritualist and thought leader Mahatria Ra*ji* says, "Fear is a strong negative emotion and limits our experiences of life. If you can conquer fear, then many wonderful experiences begin to unfold. Once you have an encounter with a tiger (biggest fear), will a small rabbit (small fear) bother you?".

One ritual I suggest is to write down all your fears on a piece of paper and burn it.

After all, most of the things we fear or worry about are imaginary; they do not happen in real life. It reminds me of what American author and humourist Mark Twain once said: "I am an old man and have seen great troubles, but most of them never happened."

If you can change your relationship with fear, you can achieve the impossible. It is important to note that fear is temporary, but giving up on your goals because of that fear has permanent consequences. Do not make it personal and limit your goals and narrow your vision. Once you get rid of this stumbling block, you will be able to fearlessly set your goals and achieve financial freedom.

If you ask me, fear has two meanings:

1. Forget Everything And Run
2. Face Everything And Rise

The choice is yours!

6. LAW OF ATTRACTION[11]

"See yourself living in abundance and you will attract it."
—Rhonda Byrne, Australian author and film producer

The law of attraction is a New Thought spiritual belief suggesting that positive thinking and actions ensure positive rewards. Author Rhonda Byrne popularized this concept through her bestselling book *The Secret*.

As American author James Redfield puts it: "Our energy flows where our attention goes." Like attracts like. If you concentrate on empowering thoughts, have inspiring goals, and have a plan of action, then it is exactly what you will manifest.

Byrne further says: "Thoughts are the primary cause of everything, and the rest is effects from those thoughts. Millionaires have become millionaires because they think thoughts of wealth."

Byrne simplifies the rules of manifestation in a three-way process called the creative process to make thoughts:

1. *Decide* what you want and then make a command to the universe. Let the universe know what you want. The universe responds to our thoughts.

2. *Believe* and *know* that you already have what you want in the unseen. Then the entire universe shifts to bringing it into the seen.

3. *Receive.*

Begin to feel wonderful about it; the way you would feel once it arrives or materializes. Feel it now. Time does not exist at the universal level. So, what you want can manifest now if your intentions are powerful enough.

To master your thoughts, Byrne recommends meditation practice for about three to ten minutes in the beginning.

Suma Varughese, former editor of *Life Positive* magazine, gives the following tips to enhance the process and make it really work:

• Practice gratitude

• Use creative visualization

• Have a vision board

Indian spiritual guru Avadhoot Baba Shivanand, in a way, corroborates this point perfectly: "When you see a beautiful home belonging to another and marvel at it and bless it, the universe or your subconscious mind gets the message that you admire and appreciate beauty. It then draws more of that into your life."

The world is as you are; it is a reflection of your inner self. Appreciation and gratitude for the abundance in life will draw the same towards you. To draw all good things into your life, you need to bless them when you see them outside.

The law of attraction is an ongoing phenomenon. Whatever you have achieved so far is what you have attracted through your subconscious mind. Only requirement is that be specific and articulate precisely what you want. State your intentions positively. Instead of saying 'I don't want to suffer', say 'I want to experience joy, I want ease'. But never be attached to the outcome and don't keep high expectations. When we are focused on an outcome, some of the energy shifts from the present into the future and deprives us from staying true to the intent and be active in the now.

Don't be impatient; believe in the process. American author and motivational speaker Wayne Dyer says, "Law of attraction is not about what you want. It is about what you are." Let us have healthy intentions. Few examples of healthy intentions are:

- I want to be a published author
- I want to travel and teach around the globe
- I want to enjoy a loving, harmonious relationship, not because I don't like the pain or incompleteness I experience now, but because I want to direct and focus my energy to this new experience

When we choose, direct, and point the mind in this way, the effort in directing the attention is coming from a wholesome and balanced place.

Indian-American author Deepak Chopra, in his book *The Seven Spiritual Laws of Success,* says, "Intention is just a thought; it's like a force in nature similar to electromagnetism." For example, if you want to heal yourself, then first of all, you must have clarity on what your intended outcome is.

Most of the top athletes will attest to this thought that after achieving a certain form through physical training and practice, it is always their mindset that gives them an edge. But here is the catch: mere having a tough mindset isn't enough. In fact, we shouldn't strain our body and mind exhaustively and end up being burned out in order to do our best. We should also understand the quality of the mental energy that is required in achieving our goals.

Dyer suggests adopting the concept of giving without expectation. He quotes the great poet Hafez:

"Even after all this time, the sun never says to the earth you owe me."

So, set your goals, get in touch with your inner core, identify your core issues, reframe them accurately, find a quiet time to say it loudly and then leave it to the universe and focus on 'Now'.

When you desire anything with all your heart, the universe conspires to helping you to achieve it.
—Paulo Coelho, Brazilian author

7. KUBERA MUDRA

From time immemorial, India has been a country rich not only in natural resources but also in learning and scholarship. The ancient science of mudras is one of the greatest and finest gifts of India to the world. This science imparts knowledge that leads to self-discovery, while providing a means to balance and maintain health independently and tap into energies of prosperity.

The mudras are symbolic or ritualistic hand gestures that are used in yoga and meditation. They create inner peace and strength; eliminate fatigue and anxiety; promote physical and emotional health; help relieve stress, depression, and anger. They calm the mind, sharpen the intellect, and promote love, happiness, prosperity and longevity.

Here, we will discuss Kubera Mudra which is relevant to our topic of financial freedom. This mudra is dedicated to Kubera—the god of wealth. As per Indian mythology, Kubera is the treasurer of the gods and famously known as the god of the riches and wealth. By practicing Kubera Mudra, one can gain wealth and success in their endeavours.

How to practice Kubera Mudra:

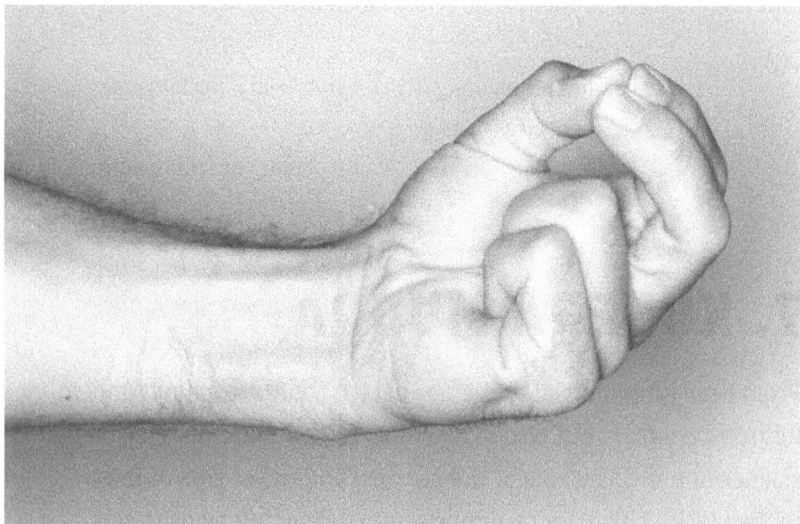

Image Source: www.lovetoknowhealth.com

Sit in a comfortable posture. Join the tips of your index finger and middle finger to the thumb. Curl the little finger and ring finger tips towards the centre of your palm. Practice this on both your hands. Remember, for this mudra, the intent is more important than the length of time.

BENEFITS:

- Improves overall health: Joining the tips of the index finger and middle fingers to the tip of the thumb balances blood pressure in the body, whereas the tips of little and ring finger touch the pressure points of solar plexus, Adrenal gland and kidneys resulting in better overall health

- Known as a wish- or goal- fulfilling mudra: Distinctly formulate the wish or goal into words, and repeat these words in your mind three times. Be sure to put slight pressure on the fingers as you practice this mudra. What you wish for may be self-centered, however, it will be fulfilled only if it brings happiness in the surroundings and society. Visualize the goal or any special wish while performing Kubera Mudra. The thought has the procreative power[12]

- Improves clarity: Helps in making day-to-day decisions like selecting a book, certain dress, or looking for specific information, etc.

- Puts more force behind plans for the future like buying a car, house, property, or finding a life partner

8. MAINTAINING YOUR PIGGY BANK

Let us understand the power of *the habit of saving.* Always remember that even ants, lizards, birds, and honey bees save for the proverbial rainy days. So, make saving money your regular practice; follow it with consistency. If you spend all your money and do not save, then how will you ever get rich? It is a game of mindset, attitude, discipline, and habit.

Think of it this way: Mount Everest is at a height of about 29,000 feet from sea level. Nobody can climb it in one go because of its difficulty level, but if one climbs 100 or 200 feet daily, one can indeed manage to achieve this feat of climbing the highest peak on this earth. Treat your habit of saving money as climbing the Everest; it's difficult because we usually have this tendency to splurge, but it's not impossible. You can save enough money if you do keep aside a set sum regularly, or even daily.

As a wealth advisor, I usually advise my clients to take baby steps. I invariably recommend them to literally maintain a piggy bank. Do not be under the impression that a piggy bank is only for kids. We, as adults, have to learn a lot from children.

So, how to start saving money in a piggy bank? Do not be in haste to buy a piggy bank from Amazon or other e-commerce sites. Use any container, jar, pouch, purse, or something that can hold a few currency notes and coins. You can also rely on apps like Gullak, Jupiter, myWisely, etc., which enable automated savings and allow you to track your progress. Make sure to be cautious and do your research well before installing the apps and setting passwords for privacy and security reasons. You can set your goals on these apps; for example, if you wish to buy a laptop, use the 'Pots' feature on Jupiter app wherein you can park your money aside from your main balance.

Besides, in some apps, you not only save money for a particular goal but also earn an interest from a linked bank account. Unless you develop a strong habit of saving, you will find plenty of ways to spend your money. Once you have selected a piggy bank, follow these *seven rules*:

1. Every member of the family must have a separate piggy bank.

2. Put a specific amount every day in your piggy bank. Quantum is not important. It is the habit that is important. It may be ₹10, ₹50, ₹100, or any amount you are comfortable keeping aside.

3. Make it a rule to never withdraw any amount from the piggy bank under any circumstances except as mentioned in point number seven below.

4. Keep your piggy bank in such a place that you can see it often.

5. Tech-savvy millennials can also try money-saving apps such as Jupiter, myWisely, as discussed above, which may be connected to your bank account.

6. Gradually reduce your expenses without compromising on your lifestyle and start saving more. For example, you can avoid branded products that are more expensive than equally good non-branded products. This will help you to save more money.

7. At the end of 30 days, pull out your savings from this piggy bank and deposit the same in your bank's recurring deposit

account or any other investment plan, which is safe and gives you a reasonable return.

Did you know ₹100 per day, if invested at 10% return per annum, will become a colossal amount of ₹3 crores in 45 years?

Always remember this timeless saying: little drops of water make the mighty ocean. Entrepreneurs and authors Manish Lath and Mukesh Kumar Agrawal share a similar thought in their book *Financial Freedom: A Promised Opportunity for You*: "Most people wait for a magical moment to drastically improve their financial conditions; realistically speaking, that never happens. If they start valuing small accruals and consistently try to improve their financial condition, only then it is bound to improve. Every drop cumulatively makes the ocean; similarly, every rupee saved and invested today will become ten after twenty years. The compounding effect takes time to show its results, but once it touches the fourth gear, it is even more exciting than winning a lottery."[13]

9. RESPECTING MONEY

We all work hard to earn money. As a working individual, you may invest in various investments and have cash reserve. No matter the financial ups and downs you go through, you should try to respect, love and nurture them. Even if you have incurred losses in some of the investments, respect it, accept it, and like it. Here are a few pointers:

- Let your purse be clean and have crisp notes. Arrange them in an order (clubbing notes of 10s, 20s, 50s, 100s, etc.) just like you would arrange your priorities on a to-do list

- Be grateful for whatever you receive. Bless it. Respect the value of other people's money as well
- Treat money as your friend, not your enemy or a liability
- Spread good energy to whatever you have by way of positive intentions and appreciation
- Maintain a record of all your cash inflows and outflows, bank balances, and liquid cash. Ensure that your books of accounts are neat and clean so that you and your money can both rest easy. When you remove clutter, you make room for more money, more abundance
- Be aware of overspending
- Remember the laws of financial freedom. Respecting money attracts more money

Repeat the following affirmations:

- I respect money
- I attract money
- I love money
- I have money

If you respect money, money will respect you. Even if you don't respect the money when you earn it, please respect it when you spend it.

Lastly, remember, what American businessman and author Robert T. Kiyosaki said, "It's not how much you make, but how much money you keep, how hard it works for you, and how many generations you keep it for."

10. DREAMING, PLANNING, AND TAKING ACTION

"When you desire something from the bottom of your heart then the whole universe conspires in helping you to achieve it."
—Paulo Coelho, Brazilian author

It is well-established that committing to a goal increases personal motivation and confidence to reach the desired destination. Goals give you a road map to follow; they give you a long-term vision and help you organize your time and resources so that you can achieve the maximum from your life.

Theoretical physicist Albert Einstein didn't speak until he was three years old. He was extremely shy and had a delayed growth as a young child. Despite this hurdle, over the years, Einstein went on to be trained as a math and physics teacher at the Swiss Federal Polytechnic School in Zurich in 1896. He may have set a goal of doing better in academics and life in general despite these shortcomings. As we are aware, he far exceeded his goal, and later on, was even awarded the Nobel Prize in Physics in 1921. Even today, Einstein is known as one of the most prominent and influential scientists of the twentieth century. Inspiring, isn't it? So, if you have a dream to be financially free or to gain a certain amount of wealth, plan ahead meticulously, and just do it despite the shortcomings in your life.

One simple exercise I want you to do is to make your small current and future balance sheet. See the following example:

Name ....
Balance Sheet as on 31.03.2024

Amount in (₹) lakhs

Capital	100.00	Assets	40.00
		Investments	30.00
		Inventory and Receivables	10.00
		Bank Balances	15.00
		Cash Balances	05.00
Total	**100.00**	**Total**	**100.00**

Don't mention liabilities or payables. Focus on capital and assets. Now make a future balance sheet the way you would like it to be. Ensure that it is challenging yet achievable and time bound.

Name ....
Balance Sheet as on 31.03.2026

Amount in (₹) lakhs

Capital	200.00	Assets	90.00
		Investments	60.00
		Inventory and Receivables	20.00
		Bank Balances	20.00
		Cash Balances	10.00
Total	**200.00**	**Total**	**200.00**

By creating a future balance sheet, you are setting a time-bound, specific, and achievable goal. Your focus should be on building capital or assets. Now, with an adequate and realistic self-image, you can also make optimal use of the unique power of your subconscious mind and your automatic goal-striving mechanism. This approach helps you develop a growth mindset. You don't need extraordinary resources; your existing resources are enough to help you achieve whatever you want in life. This is a powerful process; give it a try.

In my seminars, I give participants a specially designed 4" x 2" card (I call it the Gold Card) to instantly create their current balance sheet on one side and future balance sheet on the other. This card can be kept in your wallet, pocket or purse so you can go through it several times a day. So, go ahead and make your own Gold Card. Dream, plan, do it.

11. AFFIRMATIONS

"Setting goals is the first step in turning the invisible into the visible."
—Tony Robbins, American author and coach

The power of affirmations and visualizations has been known to us since time immemorial. The attitudes we habitually repeat become our mindset, integrating deeply into our being. To affirm is to assert convincingly that something exists and is true in any form. Your affirmations must be positive and focused on manifestations. They are essentially strings of words charged with emotion, like a river that keeps flowing. The purpose of affirmations is twofold: they either contribute to the good of the humanity or support your own spiritual growth. Remember, the punishment we got in our school time to write down something 50 times. Similarly, when we repeat something many times, it leaves imprints on our inner world. And as we know, the outer world is a reflection of the inner world.

Affirmations work best if repeated with emotion every morning and before going to bed. American inventor Thomas Edison said, "Never go to sleep without a request to your subconscious."

In *Angels Speak: Your Daily Dose of Divine Love*, author Roshani (Shenazz Nadirshah) says, "When you are repeating the affirmation out loud, you must simultaneously train your mind's eye to visualize the manifestation, feel the emotion of the intent, and inscribe it into every cell of your being. This way your entire cellular energy and body vibrates with the proclamation as if what you have affirmed is already manifested."[14]

So, start repeating affirmations from today.

AFFIRMATIONS

1. I enjoy financial freedom.
2. I always live in abundance.
3. To be rich is my birth right.
4. I need riches for my expansion and expression.
5. There are divine ways of becoming rich and I am aware of them.
6. I am a powerful money magnet.
7. My bank balance is overflowing.
8. My income is increasing on a daily basis.

9. There is a God of Miracle and I am connected with it.

10. I am open to receive limitless abundance from limitless universe.

11. I allow abundance into my life.

12. Money works for me, day and night.

13. I love to help others financially and emotionally.

14. I am already rich. I am creating wealth.

15. Becoming rich is my religious mission.

16. Universe gives me more so that I can help more and more people.

17. I am financially free and I endeavour to make others financially free.

18. I love and respect money.

CHAPTER 3

DO NOT FALL INTO A DEBT TRAP

"He who is quick to borrow, is slow to pay."
—An ancient German proverb

Peter Drucker, whose writings contributed to the philosophical and practical foundations of the modern business corporation, once famously said, "If you can't measure it, you can't manage it."

GOOD DEBT VS. BAD DEBT

Unless you measure your debts, you won't know whether they are getting better or worse. There are good debts and bad debts. Good debts might increase your wealth, while bad ones could trap you into a cycle of debt.

A debt is considered good if it meets the following conditions:

- It is used as leverage to buy appreciating assets
- It is used to expand your business, yielding a better return than the interest on the debt
- It is used to meet extreme emergencies

In our country, buying a house is often an emotional decision. The popular old saying—*"A man's home is his castle"*—can only make sense to you when you own a home. We will discuss later in the chapter whether renting a house is better than buying a house by taking out a home loan, or vice versa. For now, let's consider a home loan as a good debt. An education loan also falls into the same category. However, other loans like car loans, personal loans, credit cards loans, etc., are generally considered bad debts.

Simply put, debt is an amount of money that you owe to someone. It is a financial obligation of the debtor to his creditor. Don't be confused with nomenclatures like loans, debts, dues, outstandings, overdrafts, etc. To serve the objective of this book, all loans are treated the same. Repaying your loan is your moral, legal, and financial obligation. All the above are liabilities. The following is an indicative chart of various types of loans:

1. Home loan
2. Car loan
3. Vacation loan
4. Loan to buy gadgets
5. Personal loan
6. Mortgage loan
7. Overdraft facility from banks
8. Cash credit facility from banks
9. Term loan
10. Loan from friends and relatives
11. Marriage loan

12. Loan from private financers

13. Credit card loans

14. Gold loan

15. Loan against stocks

16. Loan against fixed deposits

17. Professional loan

18. Loan against salary

19. Loan against property

20. Bridge loan

One of the biggest flaws in taking any loan is lack of planning, budgeting, and spending on 'wants' rather than 'needs'. Food, clothing, home, education, medical treatment, etc., are the needs without which it is difficult to survive in this world. But wants are not 'needed' to survive per se; they are the things you desire or decide to buy even though you may not need them. I am not against spending on 'wants' but I am against satisfying 'wants' through borrowings. Develop a habit of writing and analyzing all your expenses. This hardly takes 10 minutes a day. Refer to the 'Expenses Matter' section of this book.

During my practice of over two decades, I have observed that almost every businessman rushes to obtain working capital loan from banks without doing proper homework. I invariably advise them to take the following steps before approaching their banker:

- Ensure that your inventory is kept at a minimum level, appropriate to the nature of your business. Piled-up and obsolete inventories are major causes of dried-up cash inflows

- Receivables must be collected promptly and professionally. Often, management grants long credit periods to customers to increase sales, which ultimately becomes a habit. What is the point of taking working capital loans when your money is already tied up with debtors for an extended period?

- Secure the maximum credit period from your suppliers. Do not purchase on an immediate payment basis just because the suppliers offer some discount

In 2022, I wrote a book titled *12 Mantras of Effortless Leadership*. I approached a major bookstore in Mumbai to buy and sell my book. The store manager negotiated with me on two things:

- What will be his commission or discount?

- The payment would be made only after the books are sold

- The store manager ensured that his investment in working capital is NIL, and by negotiating commission, he also increased his margin

- Maintain strict control on expenses which by nature increase deceptively

- Do not use working capital finance to acquire assets. The best way to finance assets is through a term loan, but ensure that the profit realized from new assets is in line with the loan repayment schedule

- If your business can generate enough cash, you will probably need minimum facilities from banks, thereby saving on huge interest costs and avoiding related hassles

The million-dollar question is: "Yes, I know debt traps are bad, but what should I do to get out of one?"

CASE STUDY

There is no one-size-fits-all formula. Much depends upon the background, ability, skills, willpower, habits, risk appetite, and willingness of a person. Let us take a practical example of a Mr. X who is heavily in debts. The first thing he must do is list out all his debts. See the following chart:

TYPE OF LOAN	GOOD OR BAD	TENURE	AMOUNTS (IN ₹)	EMI (IN ₹)	INTEREST PER ANNUM
Home loan	Good	25 years	50,00,000	37,766	7.75%
Personal loan	Bad	4 years	5,00,000	13,414	13%
Car loan	Bad	5 years	6,00,000	12,748	10%
Credit card Outstanding (3 cards)	Bad	Concurrent	3,00,000	Lump sum or minimum	36%
Pvt. financing (1)	Bad	2 years	2,00,000	Bullet payment	18%
Pvt. financing (2)	Bad	1 year	1,00,000	Bullet payment	24%
Pvt. financing (3)	Bad	1 year	75,000	Bullet payment	24%
Pvt. financing (4)	Bad	6 months	50,000	Bullet payment	24%
Pvt. financing (5)	Bad	3 months	50,000	Bullet payment	27%

My observations:

1. If we analyze the debts of Mr. X, we find that his monthly commitments are as follows:

PARTICULARS	AMOUNT (IN ₹)
1. Home loan	37,776
2. Personal loan	13,414
3. Car loan	12,748
4. Credit card (assuming 10% repayment –per month)	30,000
5. Private-financed loans (assuming 10% repayment per month)	47,500
Total	**1,41,438**

To justify the amount of ₹1,41,438 per month, the minimum net monthly income of Mr. X must be ₹2,35,000. He has violated the basic principle of finance which is your commitment towards debts must not be more than 50 to 60% of your net monthly income.

2. Mr. X has not made any budget and is a habitual borrower. He must prepare a budget right now and follow the tips given in 'Mindset' section of this book.

3. The number of lenders is too much. He has not created any emergency fund, cushion fund, reserve fund, relief fund, and so on. Without creating the above funds, applying for a car loan is a huge mistake. It's up to him how he can correct this situation. He should have created a 'vehicle fund' and waited for three years before buying a car. If a car was so important to him, he

could have purchased a second-hand car which would cost him about ₹1,00,000.

4. Credit card loans are dangerous. The same has been discussed in detail later in this book. Read it carefully and implement not only in letter but in spirit.

5. Taking personal loan clearly indicates that his cash outflow exceeds his cash inflow. Cash flow management is crucial in achieving the goal of financial freedom.

6. Taking multiple loans from private financers suggests that he is borrowing new loans to repay existing ones. This is poor financial planning.

7. He has three credit cards, and the outstanding balances are alarmingly high. No one can achieve financial freedom if they have to pay 3% to 4% interest per month on credit card debts.

8. Perhaps he is withdrawing cash from one credit card to pay the minimum amount (normally 5%) to other credit card. This practice must be avoided at all cost. Withdrawing cash using a credit card is financially reckless; it is a misuse of your finances.

9. Mr. X needs to reduce the number of loans to gain peace of mind. The order of priority for clearing debts is subjective. However, in most cases, the priority may include one or more of the following:

   a) He must drastically reduce his expenses. No more extravagant hobbies or eating out until his financial position improves. Delayed gratification is preferable to instant gratification. When I was in a debt trap, I stopped using the air conditioner in my office; I began travelling in second-class compartments in local trains, and negotiated with the lenders to reduce interest rates and extend the repayment period. At the same time, I continued to explore ways to earn additional income.

b) He can sell his car and pay off the car loan. After regaining control of his finances, he can save monthly in a 'vehicle fund' and buy a car only after there is sufficient balance in that fund.

c) He must prioritize paying off his two loans of ₹50,000 each obtained from private financers. Reducing the number of lenders gives psychological satisfaction and confidence. Generally speaking, there are three methods of handling multiple loans:

- Pay the smallest loan first

- Pay the highest interest-bearing loan first

- Pay the most bothersome loan first

d) His goal should be to clear all credit card debts on priority. A one-time settlement with credit card companies is not advisable, as it can hurt your credit score.

e) Develop at least one additional source of income.

f) Revisit the list of debts every month until you bring it to manageable level.

g) Similarly, prepare a monthly budget and allocate a specific amount to each lender. Be fair to all the lenders.

h) Focus on earning more, not just on managing debts.

i) He may consolidate his loans from private financers by convincing them that it is a win-win situation, but be careful. Consolidation solves the problem for a while. Time to repay will be stretched and amount of interest might increase.

j) If he has any additional assets like gadgets, laptops, mobiles, furniture, bicycles, bikes, etc., which he is not using, he may dispose the same to create liquidity.

k) He must ensure that he does not take on any new loans.

l) He should automate his payments by setting up ECS (Electronic Clearing Service) mandates to banks and credit card companies. With the awareness that ECS payment is going to be deducted on a particular date, Mr. X will be motivated and make all efforts to honour the same. It has worked for me. Banks usually remind in advance about the due date. Your goal-striving faculties will automatically work to help you realize your goal.

m) He can also approach credit card companies and request them to restructure the entire outstanding balance by freezing the principal amount and setting up a new installment schedule. This requires following up with the bank manager and their higher-ups. I have done this successfully with many banks like Standard Chartered, Bank of Baroda, etc. This may temporarily affect his credit score but it will provide huge relief by reducing the financial burden. If you honour your commitments, your credit score will improve later on.

n) If you are not able to honour your EMI commitments, write to the lender in advance and explain your difficulties and ask for a grace period you need. Similarly, if you receive any notice from the lenders or their advocates or any other authorities, you must respond to the same by furnishing full details of the situation you are facing. Request for a moratorium or restructuring of your loan. Many borrowers fail to reply to such notices, which is a grave mistake. Your conduct towards these authorities speaks volumes. Make it clear that you intend to pay but are facing temporary difficulties. Financial problems can be solved with financial knowledge, not just by financial help or debt.

o) Suggestions mentioned in the chapter 'Credit Cards: A Blessing or Curse' are also relevant for Mr. X.

TAKEAWAYS

Mentioned below are a few steps you may take to avoid falling into a debt trap:

1. Never have more than two credit cards (if at all you wish to have). This will ensure that you track your credit card expenses meticulously every month.

2. If you have an extra source of income, for example, bonuses, incentives, capital gains, etc., use the entire receipt in paying off your credit card dues.

3. Keep an eye on your credit score. Check your score every month at least initially. Awareness is the first step to change.

4. Don't fall prey to any no-cost EMI or zero-cost EMI options while making purchases as there are hidden costs involved in this. Lending banks normally charge processing fees and the offer is always at a higher price as discounts are available only on cash purchases.

5. Keep a portion of your income for further growth of your business or profession. If you use everything you earn in repaying, you are blocking your future growth. Be mindful of the fact that you deserve a second chance. Rework, rebuild, and repay should be your mantra.

6. Never feel guilty. Accept the reality. Forgive others as well as yourself. Never blame anybody and take full responsibility for your actions.

7. Sometimes, it makes sense to swap a high-interest loan for a low-interest one. For example, instead of paying 36% per annum to credit card companies, you may consider a personal loan that might cost you 12% to 13% per annum.

8. Do not rely solely on a single source of income. It is important to have multiple sources of income. More on this is discussed in chapter 10.

9. Did you know that if you take a home loan and pay one extra installment every year, you can complete your home loan in about 19 years instead of 25 years? How about paying one extra installment from yearly bonus, incentives, windfall, and so on?

    Further, if you increase your EMI by 5%, you can pay off 25 years' home loan in about 13 years. And, if you increase your EMI by 10%, you can pay off 25 years' home loan in only about 10 years.

10. Ask your bank to increase the interest rate spread (difference between MCLR and home loan rate offered to borrowers). The Marginal Cost of Funds based Lending Rate (MCLR) is a reference rate or internal benchmark for a financial

institution. The procedure of determining the minimum home loan interest rate is defined by the marginal code of funds-based lending rate.

A bank might agree to retain better customers if your credit score is good. Ask periodically whether there is any scope to reduce the interest rate and consider paying a larger amount upfront.

11. It is said that you must buy your freedom first, then luxuries. Nobody has become wealthy without saving and investing. Begin saving at least 10% of your monthly salary or income without fail. Make it a habit. To inculcate this habit, try using habit tracking apps like Habitify, which has helped me a lot.

12. Do not consider your one-time income as regular income. You may not be so lucky to always receive a windfall gain.

13. Identify at least one area which has the potential to derail your finances. Work on the same systematically. It may be your spending habit, reckless swiping of credit cards, or your borrowing pattern.

14. Financial freedom is more important than displaying high social status. To become rich, you need not look like a rich person.

15. One of my friends has developed a method which he likes to call 'Debt Reduction Techniques'. I personally do not subscribe to his views as they are unethical to some extent. But, if you are neck-deep in debts and the situation is so critical that it has become a question of life and death, you may go through the book (*Believe in the Power of Passive Income and Multi-Tasking* by CA Hemant Mehta and CPA Jiten Mehta) and know

how to reduce your debts. Again, I would like to emphasize that to reduce your debt by various means should be your last option. Always remember, it is your legal, ethical, and primary responsibility to repay your creditors.

"Debt is a habit. You have to change your behaviour to get out and stay out of debt."

—Dave Ramsey, American Radio personality

CHAPTER 4

CREDIT CARDS
A BLESSING OR A CURSE

"The finest advice I can give is to cut your credit card in half and throw it away."

—CA Pawan Kr Agarwal

Earning is necessary; expenses are unavoidable. No one can survive without spending on their daily needs. However, what is important here is to understand how much to spend, when, why, and where to spend.

Any expense in itself is not bad, however, an unplanned expense, if driven by emotion or erratic habit, can lead you into deep water. With plastic money and e-commerce flourishing, our spending habits have grown disproportionately. We have unwittingly normalized buying on credit. The defaulters on repayment have increased to such an extent that banks now have a separate collection or recovery department. We often read in newspapers how their recovery department harasses the defaulters. I vaguely recall having read a news article that talked about a family of four dying by suicide due to insurmountable debts. The family had several credit cards and had borrowed numerous personal loans. Unable to bear this burden of huge debts, the family members took this unfortunate and sad step.

There was a time when I had substantial outstanding on my credit cards. I set a 180 days' goal to bring the credit card bill to zero. Meanwhile, I received a reasonably large sum from a professional assignment. I cleared the entire credit card balance. It was a surreal moment—as if an enormous weight had been lifted off my shoulders. Now, I only use debit cards.

Let me quote two time-tested secrets from one of the world's wealthiest persons—Warren Buffet.

Secret Number One

Do not use a credit card. Even if you use a credit card, never avail revolving credit facility. Before you start saving, clear your credit card debts.

Secret Number Two

Invest in yourself. Be a lifelong student. Always remember that learning is earning.

BENEFITS OF CREDIT CARDS

A credit card helps you in extreme emergencies, e.g., when you must pay a medical bill or lose your job. But this shows bad planning. Medical bills can be taken care of by health or medical insurance. Similarly, you won't be affected by an unexpected layoff if you have a rainy day fund in place.

Credit cards may assist you in enhancing your credit score if they are used in a prudent and disciplined manner. It saves you from failing to honour your commitments in times of financial stress.

You could avail of discounts and bonus points. For example, you can buy flight tickets at a lower price with the help of your accumulated bonuses. It also qualifies you for a personal loan with little documentation. Credit cards come in handy if it is the last day of renewing your health insurance.

DISADVANTAGES OF CREDIT CARDS

Spending money using credit cards may prompt you to fall into a debt trap. Debit cards are a better option as you spend what you already have in your bank. If at all you apply for credit cards, make sure you vow only to use them in case of emergencies. Unfortunately, many of us lack the grit and discipline to honour that vow. Most credit card users overspend on items that are 'wants', and not 'needs'. And before they know, they are caught in a whirlwind of minimum monthly payment, and ultimately, the situation becomes critical.

One of my clients used to spend recklessly using credit cards and at the year's end, I found that his credit card spending was more than his annual income. This habit of spending more than your annual income creates a real problem while filing your income tax return because it becomes difficult to prove that your income is less than your expenditure. Hence, I advised him to use cash or debit cards. Heeding my advice, he reduced his expenses by a decent 40% in the next financial year.

When using credit cards, you should also familiarize yourself well with interest-free period credit card companies offer. However, I believe there needs to be more clarity about interest-free period. Let me give you an example of the terms and conditions of a credit card company on this interest-free (grace) period:

> *"Interest-free (grace) period will not be applicable if any balance of the previous month's bill is outstanding, even if the minimum payment due has been paid."*

On the other hand, interest on cash withdrawals using a credit card is charged from day one itself. So, check thoroughly with credit card companies the conditions (which is often written in fine print) to make use of the interest-free period.

Many people borrow on credit cards even though they have sufficient money in their bank accounts. Many of us are of the opinion that big purchases (for example, cars, laptops, etc.) should be purchased only through loans with steady EMIs. With plastic money, buying consumer goods on EMIs has become extremely convenient. Even if your bank is willing to provide you up to 80% of the value of the car, you must ask yourself "Can I save more and apply for a less amount of loan, say about 50% of the value of the car?"

If this is what you feel, then wait for a couple of years. Buy everything on credit only if you have analyzed and are sure about your payment capacity during the loan tenure. Your mantra should be: "If I can't afford to buy in cash, I must not attempt to buy on credit."

Nowadays, many banks do not even charge joining fees, annual fees, or maintenance fees. They give lifetime free credit cards. Some examples of such credit cards are the Bank of Baroda Prime Credit Card, IDFC First Wealth Credit Card, Kotak Dream Different Credit Card, HSBC

Platinum Card, Amazon Pay ICICI Bank Credit Card, InduSind Bank Credit Card, etc. However, there may be several hidden charges that many credit card users need to take seriously. Beware of the following invisible costs which naturally come with a credit card:

a) Interest and penal interest

b) Penalties

c) Over-limit charges

d) Cash withdrawal charges

e) Annual charges

f) Balance transfer charges

g) GST

h) Foreign exchange transaction charges

i) Transaction fees for certain specific payouts like booking railway tickets

j) Cheque bouncing charges, i.e., cheque return or dishonour fee

k) Legal charges

l) Charges for replacement of lost card

m) Overseas transaction charges

n) Duplicate statement fee

o) Charge slip retrieval fee

p) Outstation cheque fee

q) Fee for cash payment at branches

r) Add on card-joining and annual fees

Therefore, it is of utmost importance that you acquire a credit card with full awareness and responsibility. Once you have a credit card, use it wisely and with proper prior planning. Remember the basic rule that you must buy something only when you can genuinely afford it. This approach brings peace of mind, discipline, empowering habits, and savings. A credit card is nothing but a facility to buy things you do not need with the money you do not have.

HOW TO REDUCE YOUR CREDIT CARD OUTSTANDING TO ZERO

The most important lesson is never to pay only the minimum amount (typically 5%) each month. Doing so is a sure way to fall into a debt trap.

Even if you continue to pay only the minimum amount and don't make any fresh purchases on your credit card, it could still take over 15 years to bring the outstanding to zero. Isn't that shocking? Even if you increase the minimum payment from 5% to 10%, it will only help you marginally. My advice is that you take one of the following steps:

i)   Determine once and for all that you want to get rid of your credit card debt.

ii) Set a timeline within which you want to achieve this goal. It may be 12 months or any other timeframe that suits you, provided it is challenging.

iii) Suppose you want to clear your credit card debt in 12 months. Use an EMI calculator to determine how much you should pay monthly to clear the debt within that period.

iv) If your outstanding is ₹1,00,000 you must pay ₹10,046 per month (p.m.) to clear the same in 12 months.

Similarly, you will need to pay ₹7,271 p.m. to clear the same in 18 months.

And you will need to pay ₹5,905 p.m. to clear the same in 24 months.

Credit Card Loan

Outstanding ₹1,00,000

Interest 36% p.a.

EMI for 12 months = ₹10,046 p.m.
(Total payments ₹1,20,555)

EMI for 18 months = ₹7,271 p.m.
(Total payments ₹1,30,876)

EMI for 24 months = ₹5,905 p.m.
(Total payments ₹1,41,714)

Second alternative:

Negotiate with your bank. The bank might agree to convert your outstanding into convenient equal monthly installments (EMIs).

Third alternative:

If eligible, you may take a personal loan of ₹1,00,000 and clear the credit card outstanding. The interest rate on a personal loan might be 11% to 13%, while on a credit card outstandings, you pay 36% or more. Whatever solution you choose, please ensure it does not become a habit. Your objective should be to attain financial freedom and eliminate all bad loans.

On personal loan, your EMIs will be as follows:

PERSONAL LOAN

Outstanding ₹1,00,000

Interest 12% p.a.

EMI for 12 months = 8,885 p.m.
(Total payments ₹1,06,619)

EMI for 18 months = ₹6,098 p.m.
(Total payments ₹1,09,768)

EMI for 24 months = ₹4,707 p.m.
(Total payments ₹1,12,976)

You will save ₹13,936 in 12 months, ₹21,108 in 18, and ₹28,738 in 24 months.

Fourth alternative:

Many people, mostly the elderly, are emotionally attached to their liquid investments like fixed deposits, recurring deposits, and investments in mutual funds, which hardly yield 6% to 8% interest per annum. Similarly, they might have investments in precious metals like gold and silver where the percentage of returns may often be in single digits. At the same time, they are enjoying revolving credit facilities on which they pay interest of 36% or more per annum.

This is like borrowing at a 36% interest rate and investing in instruments that fetch 6% to 9% p.a. This makes no sense, and in fact, it is dangerous. Liquidate your investments, pay off your credit card debts, and start saving and investing afresh. Remember to create an emergency fund.

Fifth alternative:

You may get interest-free loans from your friends and relatives. Sometimes your employer may give you an interest-free loan.

Clear the credit card outstanding balance with this loan and start paying those who provided you an interest-free loan.

Sixth alternative:

If you have numerous credit cards, try to clear outstanding of some of them. It can be done if you diligently cut down your expenses. It will give you confidence and some leeway in transferring balances from other credit cards. However, a balance transfer is only a temporary solution as it might affect your credit score. It would help if you enquire whether your credit card is eligible for a balance transfer and what the processing charges are.

Seventh alternative:

Reduce your expenses. If you spend more on your 'wants' than your 'needs', you must closely monitor your expenses. Make a budget and compare it with your actual expenses. Refer to the earlier part of this chapter and learn how to create a reserve fund and emergency fund and implement the lessons you have learned. Spending more than your income is a financial sin.

Eighth alternative:

If you are a first-time credit card owner and have no credit score, apply for a secured credit card. This means you keep an equivalent amount in a fixed deposit as security for issuing the credit card, and your sanction limit equals the fixed deposit amount. You earn interest on the fixed deposit while paying through the automated payment system.

Even if you don't have a secured credit card, follow the same system and use your credit cards only when you have an equivalent amount in your saving account. Since credit card companies give a grace period of 30 to 45 days to pay the outstanding balance, you might earn some interest on your fixed deposit and avoid falling into a debt trap.

A fearless consumer advocate and an American legal scholar Elizabeth Warren rightly advises: "Treat credit cards like what they are; little plastic grenades that must be handled very carefully."

CHAPTER 5

EXPENSES MATTER

"Beware of little expenses. A small leak will sink a great ship."
—Benjamin Franklin, *American statesman*

Today, we all are living in the age of consumerism. Advertisements in various media continue to brainwash us. Manufacturers know our weaknesses. With plastic money easily accessible and consumer loans given at the drop of a hat, we are tempted to buy products that, under normal circumstances, we can't afford. We buy with the expectation of our future income. We have forgotten the difference between our 'wants' and 'needs'. I am not suggesting that one should not buy luxury products, but prudence demands that first, we must earn and save and then buy luxuries. Frugality is the mantra one should always remember to achieve financial freedom.

Before buying luxury and status products, ask yourself the following questions:

1. Do I really *need* it?
2. Can I afford to buy the same in cash?
3. Do I have a complex buying behaviour?

4. What if I buy this product next year?

5. Is it in sync with my goal of financial freedom?

6. Have I created an emergency fund before deciding to buy this product?

7. Is it a depreciating asset or an appreciating asset?

8. Most of us buy luxury items to have a sense of accomplishment. It triggers the release of dopamine, a feel-good hormone. Can you find alternative sources of feeling good?

9. What difference it will make if you buy a small car (or a used car) instead of a luxury car?

10. Do you really need branded goods?

11. Do you buy luxury items to show off that you are better than your friends, colleagues, or neighbours?

12. When you see an advertisement that says "You must have," ask yourself a counter question: How do you know that?

13. What percentage of features of your cell phone do you usually use?

14. Do you really need a new cell phone?

15. Do you love to shop?

16. Are you a shopaholic?

17. Have you ever made a budget for your expenses?

Overspending is the result of purchasing without thinking. The sword of inflation is always hanging over our heads. Do not become a part of show business. It invites more problems. Taking timely action can control your expenses.

So, here is my six-step guide to managing, controlling, and planning your expenses:

1. Beware of your spending habits
2. Be cost-conscious
3. Budget and account for every expense
4. Negotiate your bills
5. Catch them young
6. Specimen for recording expenses

1. SPENDING HABITS

"I'd like to live as a poor man with lots of money."
—Pablo Picasso, Spanish painter and sculptor

Beware of your spending habits. If you invest wisely, even a small amount of ₹100 per day can grow into a million rupees in 20 years. Earning money is meaningless if you do not spend it wisely. Some of my staff members always grumble and ask for an advance in the last week of the month. They invariably have two mobile phones, and their spending habits are simply horrible.

Most of us need a budget for spending. We often spend on an ad hoc basis, impulsively. It is said that a budget does not restrict your freedom—it gives you direction. Either you control the money, or it will control you. Once you have a budget, you know where to spend and where not to spend. As the American radio personality Dave Ramsey says, "A budget is telling your money where to go instead of wondering where it went."

Keep track of all your expenses, however small they may be. List out all your expenses, every day, every week, and every month. Compare it with your budget. Either you change the budget or your spending habits. Awareness is more critical than actual spending. Awareness, when followed by action, produces results.

Another important reason for having an eye on spending money is that expenses, by nature, grow rapidly. Gadgets become outdated; new ones come with a higher price. Hotels and restaurants are increasing their tariffs every year. Inflation is affecting us constantly. New products are coming into the market on a daily basis to make existing products obsolete.

Abhishek, aged about 42, is an executive in a limited company. His gross package is about ₹18 lakhs per annum, and his monthly living expenses are about ₹50,000 per month. I gave him the shocking news that his monthly expenses will shoot up to ₹4,00,000 per month in 2040, when he will probably retire. ₹4 lakhs per month after retirement, with no job (or at most a part-time job), was enough to make him sit up straight, square his shoulders, and widen his eyes. With astonishment and surprise, he uttered: "Is it true?"

Yes, your living and essential expenses will increase by 9% to 12% per annum, whether you like it or not. See the following table:

YEAR	EXPENSES PER MONTH IN (₹)
2022	50,000
2028	1,00,000
2034	2,00,000
2040	4,00,000

(Compounded at 12% per annum. However, this is only indicative. Actual figures may differ based on circumstances.)

Let us examine the effect of inflation in a realistic manner.

The following chart depicts how your expenses will increase at different rates of inflation:

Monthly Expenses

YEAR	ESTIMATED RATE OF INFLATION				
	6%	7%	8%	10%	12%
2023	50,000	50,000	50,000	50,000	50,000
2028	66,911	70,128	73,466	80,526	88,117
2033	89,542	98,358	1,07,946	1,29,687	1,55,292
2038	1,19,828	1,37,952	1,58,608	2,08,862	2,73,678
2043	1,60,357	1,93,484	2,33,048	3,36,375	4,82,315
2048	2,14,594	2,71,372	3,42,424	5,41,735	8,50,003

This is simple mathematics. You will need a minimum ₹2,14,594 per month by 2048 to maintain the same lifestyle having the same essential expenses, in case the inflation rate is 6% per annum. If the rate is 12% per annum, your expenses by 2048 will be ₹8.5 lakhs per month.

Of course, your income may also grow in the same pattern. But regular income may stop or be considerably reduced at a certain point. So, to meet your expenses (wants or needs), you must have an adequate corpus that will generate passive income to meet your 'wants' and 'needs' till you survive.

The next time you want a new iPhone or even a branded shirt, consider whether you *need* it or *want* it. Remember the famous phrase by the American statesman Benjamin Franklin: *"A penny saved is two pence clear."*

Start tracking your daily, monthly, and quarterly expenses. This is simple yet powerful, but unfortunately, most of us grossly ignore this important habit. By tracking your expenses, you can reduce them by 10% to 15% or even more. Let expense tracking become your habit—you will never regret it.

Sushiil Mehta, founder of Jains Car Shoppe in Chennai, had quite a humble beginning. Back then, he was assisting his father in their 200-square-foot office space. Today, he has over two-lakh square feet of operating space, 25 showrooms, and 700-plus employees. He narrates an incident about the values of money his father, Omprakash Mehta, taught him in his early days. He recalls that one day, while tallying the cash earned for the day, he was short by ₹10. He tallied it multiple times, but there was still a gap. He told his father there was a difference, but it was so small that it did not matter.

Immediately, his father corrected him and said sternly, "Son, please remember, today it is just a matter of ₹10, tomorrow it

> will be millions! No matter what, we must ensure that the money adds up and that accounts are in order. Do not ever close shop for the day unless this is done." And, of course, he made Sushiil stay back until they solved the mystery of the missing ₹10.
>
> At that time, Sushiil wondered why his father fussed so much on such a small thing. However, in the years to come, its impact on his life and business was profound. From his father, he learned the value of money. Whether it was small or in abundance, it was necessary to value this precious resource and never be careless. To account for it and be accountable for it.[15]

One of my clients, a financer, never lends money to a person who displays a high social status. According to him, such people are quick to borrow but slow to repay. They spend only with the expectation of getting more money in the future. Another important point he mentioned was that if a person has too many credit cards, he will avoid lending money to that borrower. Thirdly, he invariably checks the bank statements of the first-time borrower. Even if a single cheque has bounced during the past three to six months, that borrower cannot become his client.

On frugality and spending wisely, the best book I have ever read is, *The Millionaire Next Door* by Thomas J. Stanley and William D. Danko. If you have not read this book, I suggest you grab it and read it. The authors state that financial independence is more important than displaying high social status. You are not what you drive. They further mention that you can learn a great deal about affluent people by studying their vehicle-buying habits. For example, most millionaires are dealer shoppers rather than dealer loyalists. How about buying a second-hand car? It has been observed that those who buy second-

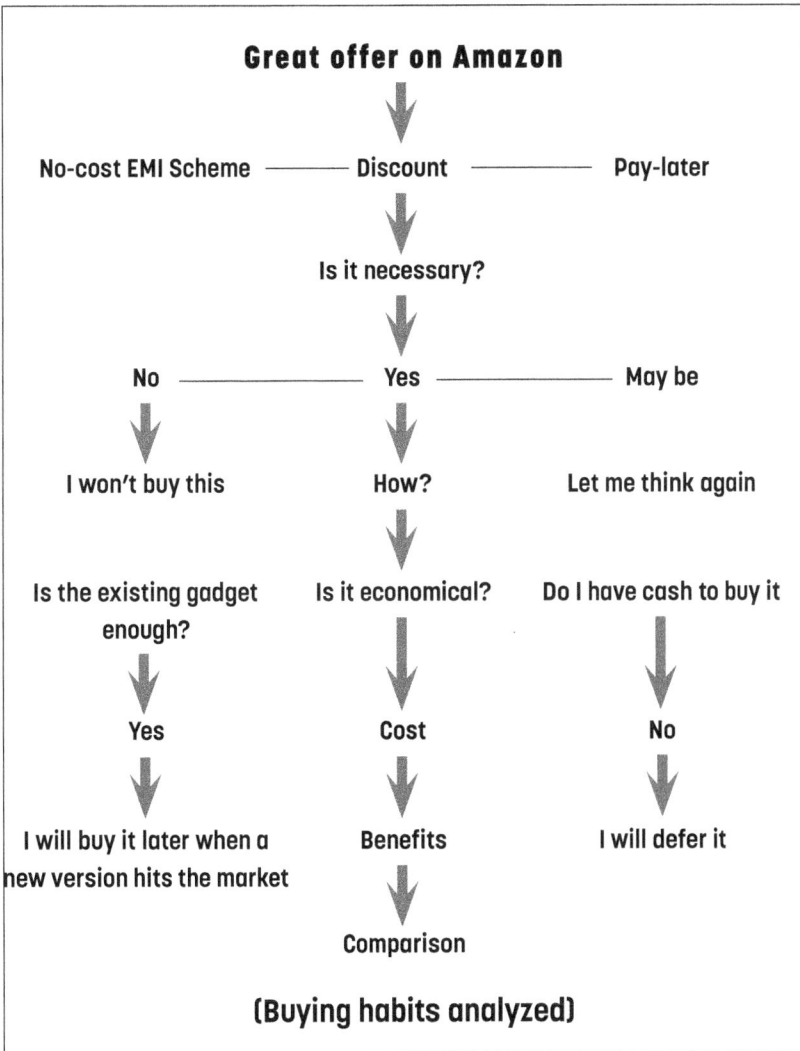

Great offer on Amazon

No-cost EMI Scheme ——— Discount ——— Pay-later

Is it necessary?

No ——— Yes ——— May be

I won't buy this / How? / Let me think again

Is the existing gadget enough? / Is it economical? / Do I have cash to buy it

Yes / Cost / No

I will buy it later when a new version hits the market / Benefits / I will defer it

Comparison

(Buying habits analyzed)

hand cars are calculative in every area of their life. The point is that one should not buy a luxurious car. The fact is, can you wait till you become reasonably wealthy? Never buy any luxury item in anticipation of becoming rich.

You should observe a non-spending day once a month. On this day, no spending on your 'wants', for example, no cigarettes, no alcohol, no cab, no eating outside, no movies, no shopping, and of course, no charity. Carry only minimum amount in your wallet that is absolutely necessary. You may also follow one or two rituals as mentioned in the chapter of *Mindset*. This will convey to your subconscious that wealth is created by earning more and spending less.

> *"We make ourselves rich by making our wants few."*
> —Henry David Thoreau, American naturalist and essayist

2. BE COST-CONSCIOUS

One of the guiding principles of Narayana Murthy, founder of Infosys, has always been to be cost-conscious. He followed cost-consciousness by actively demonstrating the same.

By living simply and thinking deeply, he set an example for others to follow. It is said that he rode his bicycle all the way to meet his very first customer. His remarkable aspect was his simplicity, an essential part of who he was—not just an appearance. The Murthys did not own a television set until their son was 12 years old. He still does not wear expensive designer suits or travel by first class—he flies economy! He lives in Bangalore with his wife Sudha in their modest three-bedroom flat on Hosur Road. These values naturally filtered down from the top and soon became an integral part of the company.[16]

Here are a few more exemplary cases. Despite being one of the richest individuals in the country, Azim Premji of WIPRO has shown little interest in luxuries. He prefers to travel by economy class, doesn't own expensive cars, and prefers to stay in the company's guest house during business trips. He loves to have food from the company's canteen.

Late Indian businessman G.D. Birla had once emphasized to his young son Basant Kumar to 'never utilize' wealth solely for fun and frolic, to spend the bare minimum on oneself, and to deride 'worldly pleasures.' Such austere behaviour was taken to great lengths. He advised to the younger generation to exercise restraint in food consumption, never consume alcohol or tobacco, wake up early in the morning, and avoid extravagance.

This personal frugality was also carried over into financial management practices at the workplace. The centuries-old 'partha system'[17] perfected by traditional Marwari traders, which involved accounting for cash and credit at the end of each business day, was modernized by G.D. Birla to run his industrial enterprises. Of course, in a large global conglomerate, it might be challenging to follow such a system, but its core principles continue to be reflected in the daily reporting practices and strict prudence in tracking financial flows.

American investor and philanthropist Warren Buffet lives in a modest house, does not spend on big cars or entertainment, and believes that the ultimate luxury is in doing what he loves to do every day.

3. BUDGETING AND ACCOUNTING

I am a practicing Chartered Accountant, I analyze, study, and audit historical accounts. Proper accounting provides a clear understanding of where the money has come from and where it has been spent. It helps us realize what our past failures and achievements are, which is crucial because you cannot control what you cannot measure. However, knowing the past is only useful if we learn from it and move forward.

We also prepare projected accounts, commonly known as budgeting or forecasts. These projections become our goals. Then comes planning, action, and execution. To me, for a venture to be successful, its accounting must have all the following elements:

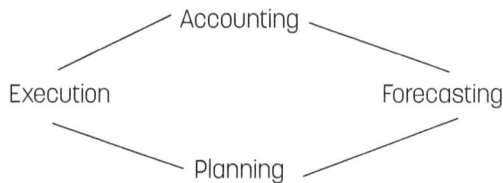

```
                    Accounting
          Execution              Forecasting
                     Planning
```

Accounting reveals our debts, cash inflows, cash outflows, income, expenditures, assets, and liabilities. It reflects our capital and reserves. Remember the six types of reserves:

- Revenue Reserve
- Capital Reserve
- Capital Redemption Reserve

- Securities Premium Reserve
- Debenture Redemption Reserve
- Revaluation Reserve

For individuals, I recommend the following reserves:

- Emergency fund
- Reserve fund
- Cushion fund
- Special reserves

These reserves help individuals to identify their unhealthy spending habits, bad debts, and areas that require special attention. Budgeting or forecasting can be done monthly, quarterly, or yearly. By comparing your actual expenses with your forecasts, you can align your finances with your goals.

There are controllable and uncontrollable expenses. Only proper accounting enables you to manage the controllable ones and prepare for the uncontrollable ones. Accounting is not rocket science; even a layperson can do it. It is only at the forecasting stage that you need vision. A thumb rule of effective budgeting is first to analyze your past accounting and then set goals for the future.

Always keep in mind the following:

1. Are your bad debts reducing month by month?
2. Is the interest you pay to lenders reasonable?
3. Are your expenses on 'needs' adequately planned?
4. Are you saving and investing at least 10% of your income?

5. Have you have made provisions for a sinking fund (specific-purpose fund), for example, buying a car or going on a vacation?

6. Are you overspending and using credit cards to buy things you may not need?

7. Are your family and business partners consulted when making a budget?

8. Do you have too many mortgages or consumer loans?

9. Do you spend your time, money, energy, and effort in financial planning to ensure a life free from financial worries?

10. Do you have more than one car? Do you really need your second or third car?

Operate your personal life or business with a well-thought-out budget. No budget signifies no plan, defined goals, or clear-cut direction.

4. NEGOTIATE YOUR BILLS

It is said that everything in this world is negotiable. Have you ever visited a renowned lawyer's office? You might immediately notice their lavish lifestyle—the five-star culture in their office, splendid interior, gorgeous staff welcoming you, large conference room, and all the comforts you can imagine in a five-star resort in Goa. All these amenities are costly. So, how does the lawyer afford them? Of course, the cost is built into the bills you receive and the fees you pay to the lawyer. If you look around hard enough, you might also find an equally competent lawyer who would charge you half the amount. You have two options:

1. Negotiate (even though you are not likely to succeed)
2. Find another lawyer

This lawyer might be appropriate for you if you represent a large corporation with a complex organizational hierarchy. But, for others, being cost-conscious pays.

This is not about lawyers alone. Even accountants, insurance advisors, portfolio managers, doctors, fitness consultants, and many others fall into the same category. You have a right to negotiate as a customer or client or consumer. Why not negotiate when you buy a laptop, refrigerator, or an air conditioner. The other party needs you much more than you need them.

Recently, I purchased a Honda Amaze. After finalizing everything, I asked the salesperson about discounts. Initially, he refused to offer any, but after some persuasion, the salesperson agreed to provide free insurance and seat cover.

You must save wherever you can, whether it is as small an expense as buying from a grocery supplier or chemist, or as big an expense as booking a hotel. One of my friends told me he gets a considerable discount on doctors' consultation fees or bills in big corporate hospitals.

Spending habits are often the result of our ego, empathy, and altruism. It is deeply personal, emotional, individualistic, and shaped on our past beliefs and upbringing. Do remember that spending money on 'wants' always depends on your subconscious mindset and not on logic.

Expenses matter even in your investments, whether in mutual funds, stocks, or insurance. When you invest for the long term, the fees and commissions payable to intermediaries every year can be substantial, the return on investment is adversely affected, and so is the corpus you receive from your investment. Therefore, buying financial products directly from companies under direct schemes is prudent. The same can now be quickly done through online purchases. Similarly, while selecting a fund, do not ignore the expense ratio. Those who spend more cannot give you more.

Your investment compounds over time, and so do the expenses, which may prove costly, affecting your retirement fund and return on investment. Please remember that passive funds (for e.g., index funds) have lower expenses than active funds. (Refer to the chapter on Equities and Mutual Funds for more insights.)

5. CATCH THEM YOUNG

Money management has never been a part of the school curriculum. Therefore, it becomes necessary for us to teach our children and younger generation the art of managing money. We have already discussed the importance of a piggy bank—this could be a good beginning. Teach them the difference between good spending habit and emotional spending. Link their savings to a goal. In my school days, I was able to buy a bicycle from the savings I accumulated from my pocket money. Explain the importance of saving money to children. Please encourage them to save for emergencies or events like birthdays, sports, etc. Even if they don't understand the importance of the Li Ka-Shing's budget model (explained further in this chapter) at this stage, it will be of immense use in the future.

One of my clients—let us call him Prince—was successful in business and amassed enormous wealth. At the time of his death by accident, he owned thirteen immovable properties. He never taught his only child, Simon, the value of frugality, saving, and investing. To maintain his lifestyle, Simon sells one of the properties every year. Is there any doubt that soon he is going to become bankrupt?

The most important gift you can give your children is not financial help or expensive gifts, but the following:

- Inculcate a habit of spending wisely
- Instill confidence in them so that they can stand on their own feet
- Teach them leadership traits and money management skills
- Teach them discipline and the importance of hard work
- In short, do not give them a fish; teach them how to fish. When you give them a fish, you feed them for a while, but when you teach them how to fish, you feed them for life

Remember to teach them the GEM theory; they would love it.

- **G**row your money
- **E**arn more money
- **M**anage your money

Inculcating saving habits in kids, students, and teenagers is essential.

They reach the age where they get some pocket money to spend; this is the time when they can pick up good money habits. Here, the risk is minimal and controllable.

Below are a few steps that might help:

1. The first step is to develop a habit of saving through the piggy bank, as you learned in the '*Mindset*' chapter. Put a sticker on the piggy bank that says: "I love saving."

2. Teach them the difference between 'wants' and 'needs'. Whenever they want to purchase something, let them ask themselves, "Is it a 'want' or 'need'?"

3. Children must know the benefits of saving at their respective ages. Show them the benefit of compounding. It is necessary to fix a percentage of savings. Don't go overboard—5% of saving is a good start, which can be increased gradually and consistently.

4. Let them set a goal. For example, "I want to celebrate my birthday," which falls six to nine months from today. You may also set a medium-term goal from one to three years.

5. Monitor their spending habits. Children want to buy every new thing they see. Alert them about overspending and emotional spending. Kids must know not to be influenced by T.V., social media ads, etc. Once they know the difference between 'wants' and 'needs' and the emotional aspect of purchasing, they will become cost-conscious when they grow older.

6. Saving habits will automatically instill discipline, confidence, and goal-setting mindset.

7. Open a savings bank account in the child's name. Some banks also provide debit cards to children above ten years. The Reserve Bank of India has also issued guidelines allowing children above ten years to operate bank accounts independently to promote financial inclusion and bring uniformity in opening saving bank accounts in the children's name.

8. Children should be taught to maintain how much they have received, spent, and saved. A small notebook is enough. Alternatively, they might also use apps like Wallet. (Children these days are quite tech-savvy.)

9. Teach them the importance of helping others. Inculcate a habit of contributing a certain percentage of their pocket money to charity.

10. The beauty of teaching children is that you will also learn many things and become more disciplined.

11. Teach them how to respect and value money.

12. Clearly explain the importance of keeping an emergency fund. For example, your child may have to hire a public transport on its way back home from school in case of heavy rains if the school bus is unavailable.

13. College students must explore the possibility of working part-time to ensure an additional source of income (apart from the pocket money they receive). They might creatively think out of the box to reduce expenses and increase revenue without compromising their studies.

14. Teach them the importance of a debt-free life and disadvantages of credit cards. They need the discipline and an awareness of the importance of building a good credit score.

15. Lastly, remember to lead by example.

"95% of everything you do is the result of habit."
—Aristotle, Greek philosopher and polymath

6. SPECIMEN FOR RECORDING EXPENSES

By now, you understand the importance of recording expenses. You should maintain a notebook to record your:

- Daily expenses
- Monthly expenses
- Quarterly expenses
- Yearly expenses
- Emergency expenses

The tables provided at the end of this section are indicative and not exhaustive. They are designed to help you create a system that suits your needs.

During my 25 years of practice, I have advised my clients to record their expenses. Unfortunately, most do not maintain these records properly; some believe it is time-consuming and a waste of effort. However, those who have followed my advice reported that they have reaped tremendous financial benefits. Many have reduced their expenses by 10% to 20%. Unless you write down your expenses, you cannot track them, and therefore, cannot eliminate unnecessary costs. When you focus on the better use of money, you can naturally achieve your financial goals.

When recording expenses, you need to decide whether a particular expense is a (1) need or (2) want. These categories should be listed in the relevant columns so that you have better control over unnecessary spending. I also suggest including a third column called 'Target.' It is something other than your plan of action to track useless expenses.

Drill that into your mind that every expense should first be classified into two categories: 'need' and 'want.' Then, review it and ask yourself if it can be reduced or eliminated. That becomes your *target*. If there is no room for reduction, note this in the target column.

Writing down daily expenses will take about 10 minutes each day. Similarly, recording monthly expenses will take 15 minutes each month, and quarterly expenses will take 10 to 15 minutes each quarter. And ultimately, writing your yearly expenses will take, at most, half an hour. Is that too much to ask? I promise that once you develop this habit, you will notice tremendous improvement in controlling of your finances.

Table A
My Daily Expense Sheet

PARTICULARS	NEEDS	WANTS	MY TARGET
Conveyance			
Restaurants			
Stationary			
Smoking			
Other addictions			
Purchases a. Online b. Offline			
Newspapers			
Magazines			
Gifts			
Salons/ beauty parlours			
Eating at street food joints			
Medicines			
Doctors			
Legal expenses			
Movies			
OTT and other subscriptions			
Donations			
Penalties			
Interest			

PARTICULARS	NEEDS	WANTS	MY TARGET
Clothing			
Fun			
Charity			
Education			

Total of Wants (A) ....

Total of Needs (B) ....

Total of wants and needs (A+B) ....

Target amount (C) ....

Potential saving (A+B)-C ....

Summary of Daily Expenses
(at the end of a particular month)
For the month of .... and for the year ....

	MONTHLY	YEARLY
Wants		
Needs		
Target		
Potential savings (A+B)-C		

Notes:
- Record your daily expenses separately for at least 30 days.

Table B
My Monthly Expense Sheet
(not included in Table A)

PARTICULARS	NEEDS	WANTS	MY TARGET
Rent			
Maintenance/ society charges			
Grocery			
Milk			
Vegetables			
Newspapers			
Clothing			
Wages / salaries (1) (2) (3)			
Mobile recharge			
Internet			
Repairs (1) (2) (3)			
Electricity			
LPG consumption			
EMIs			

PARTICULARS	NEEDS	WANTS	MY TARGET
Credit card bills			
Bank charges			
Late fees / penalties			
Medical expenses			
Education			
Vehicle maintenance			
Petrol /diesel			

Summary of Monthly Expenses
For the month of .... and for the year ....

	MONTHLY	YEARLY
Wants (A)		
Needs (B)		
Target (C)		
Potential savings (A+B)-C		

Table C
My Quarterly Expense Sheet
(not included in Table A or B)

PARTICULARS	NEEDS	WANTS	MY TARGET
Insurance (1) (2) (3)			
Medical expenses			
Short vacations			
Religious visits			
Guests			
Ceremonies			
Gadgets			

Summary of Quarterly Expenses
For the quarter ended .... and for the year ....

	QUARTERLY	MONTHLY	YEARLY
Wants (A)			
Needs (B)			
Target (C)			
Potential savings (A+B)-C			

Table D
My Yearly Expense Sheet
(not included in Table A, B, or C)

PARTICULARS	NEEDS	WANTS	MY TARGET
Insurance (1) (2) (3)			
Medical check-up			
Vacations			
Education			
Repairs and maintenance			
Bonuses and incentives			
Celebrations			
Computers, laptops, and other gadgets			
Taxes			
Consultancy charges			
Total			

Table E
My Emergency Expense Sheet
(Not recorded in table A, B, C and D)

PARTICULARS	NEEDS	WANTS	MY TARGET
Doctors			
Hospitals			
Sickness			
Vehicle expenses			
Family functions			
Religious trips			
Unexpected excursions			

Summary of my emergency expenses

PARTICULARS	NEEDS	WANTS	MY TARGET
Annual emergency expenses (Wants) (A)			
Needs (B)			
Target (C)			
Potential savings (A+B)-C			

My annual emergency expenses (Total of needs and wants)	
My estimated monthly emergency expenses	

Notes:
1. Write down all your daily expenses, however small they may be.
2. Count the money in your purse in the morning and check what remains when you retire for the day. The difference should be reflected in your daily expenses.
3. Initially, for at least 30 days, you must write down all your expenses. Later on, try using an app like Wallet or an appropriate technology to help you record and track your expenses against a predetermined budget.
4. Here's a challenge for you—can you reduce your daily average expenses by 20%? Believe me, some of my friends and clients have reduced their expenses by more than 30%. Remember, if invested wisely, ₹100 per day becomes a million rupees in 20 years.
5. The tables provided above are only indicative. You may prepare your own table.
6. Focus on the target area and find ways to reduce expenses.

Table F
My Total Monthly Expense Sheet

PARTICULARS	NEEDS	WANTS	MY TARGET
Total monthly expenditures from Table A			
Total monthly expenses from Table B			
Total monthly expenses from Table C			

PARTICULARS	NEEDS	WANTS	MY TARGET
Total monthly expenses from Table D			
Total average monthly expenses from Table E			
Total A+B+C+D+E			
Total monthly expenses on needs and wants			

Study and monitor Table F carefully. Many of us do not yet to know our average monthly expenses or outflows. Once you know your actual monthly expenses, you can set your goal accordingly. More importantly, you will understand whether your average monthly income is sufficient to meet your average monthly expenses. If not, you need to work seriously on increasing your income, reducing expenses, generating additional sources of income, and saving wherever possible.

Many of my clients are not clear about their actual expenses. Once you complete this exercise, you will be surprised to see your actual financial position and identify the areas where you are stuck. Believe me, this will be an eye-opening exercise for you.

LI KA-SHING BUDGET MODEL

Nicknamed 'Superman', Li Ka-Shing is one of the most influential entrepreneurs in Asia. He lives a balanced, simple, and inspiring life.

The Li Ka-Shing budget model is based on a simple allocation model. This model allocates one's income in five parts:

Living expenses	30%
Interpersonal relationship (networking)	20%
Investments	25%
Leisure and travel	10%
Learning and self-development	15%
Total	100%

The percentage of allocation will vary from person to person, but the model mentioned above will serve as a guide on your journey toward financial freedom. What is important is that you allocate a certain percentage to each of the five parts of the model. There are various methods of allocation. Adopt the one which suits you best, and follow it consistently.

Following the Li Ka-Shing model, allocate 30% to your household requirements. (This percentage might increase if your income is low). Then, reserve 20% for interpersonal relationships, 15% for self-development, and 10% for vacations. However, ensure that you invest 25% of your income in bonds, shares, metals, fixed deposits, etc. Your investment strategy depends on your age, risk appetite, financial goals, and family background.[18]

Allocating 25% for investments may seem high at first glance. But remember, this is necessary to meet future requirements, such as education, your children's marriage, buying property, emergencies like lockdowns or layoffs, and for your initial investments if at all you want to start a new venture. It's crucial to have a *corpus* at the time of retirement. Start with an amount you are comfortable with and gradually move towards meeting the 25% investment target.

My advice is to invest first and then manage all other expenses from whatever remains.

> *"A wealthy mindset minimizes expenses in self-entertainment and maximizes investments in self-education."*
>
> —Orrin Woodward, American author

CHAPTER 6

HAVE A COMPOUNDING FAMILY

"Little disciplines compounded over time make a huge difference"
—Albert Einstein, Theoretical physicist

Imagine all the members of your family—parents, children, grandchildren, grandparents—earning together and contributing to the wealth of the family. If there are two grandchildren and two children, then you have additional members earning for the family. Today, in the age of nuclear families, this seems startling but in the world of compounding, it is possible. Compounding ensures that:

a) Capital or corpus is growing

b) Dividends (returns) are received

c) Returns are invested

d) Returns yield returns

e) All returns are invested

The following example explains what compounding is through a metaphor of a compounding family. Here, the grandparent makes a one-time investment of ₹10 lakhs which yields 10% return per annum and the same is handed over to the next senior member of the family. The total corpus accumulated in the next 10 years will look as follows:

YEAR	GRAND-PARENT	PARENT	CHILD (1)	CHILD (2)	GRAND-CHILD (1)	GRAND-CHILD (2)	TOTAL
1	10,00,000	-		-	-	-	10,00,000
2	10,00,000	1,00,000	-	-	-	-	11,00,000
3	10,00,000	2,00,000	10,000	-	-	-	12,10,000
4	10,00,000	3,00,000	30,000	1,000	-	-	13,31,000
5	10,00,000	4,00,000	60,000	4,000	100	-	14,64,100
6	10,00,000	5,00,000	1,00,000	10,000	500	10	16,10,510
7	10,00,000	6,00,000	1,50,000	20,000	1,500	61	17,71,561
8	10,00,000	7,00,000	2,10,000	35,000	3,500	217	19,48,717
9	10,00,000	8,00,000	2,80,000	56,000	7,000	589	21,43,589
10	10,00,000	9,00,000	3,60,000	84,000	12,600	1,348	23,57,948

So, the amount of ₹10 lakhs compounded at 10% per annum becomes ₹23.6 lakhs in 10 years, as six pairs of hands are working.

This is just the tip of the iceberg. ₹10 lakhs compounded at 10% per annum becomes a colossal amount of ₹1.74 crores in about 30 years!

WHAT IS COMPOUNDING?

Simply put, compounding is the increase in the value of an investment due to both the interest earned on the principal and the accumulated interest that has already been earned. It is a plan for making your money work for you and can be seen as a powerful way to grow wealth. You can plan for long-term goals, like retirement, by harnessing the power of compounding.

Let's look at something interesting:

Take a large sheet of paper, say A2 size, which is about 16.5 inches by 23.4 inches. Now, fold it once. This will reduce the paper's surface area by half. Again, fold this folded paper. The surface area of the paper will be now one fourth of the original paper. Keep on folding it as many times as you can. If you have managed to fold it 26 times, then the size of the paper would be taller than Mount Everest. At the moment, a California High School student holds the world record. He or she was able to fold a very large piece of tissue paper 12 times. It seems impossible, but it's true. Compounding is like folding a piece of paper over and over again.

HOW DOES IT WORK?

To give you another example, think of compounding as a Chinese bamboo tree. When the seed of this tree is sown, there are no visible signs of growth in the first four years. Patience is tested, and we start to wonder whether our efforts will bear fruits. But in the fifth year, you will notice a massive growth—the Chinese bamboo tree grows to about 25 meters in just two months. The parable of the Chinese bamboo tree teaches us invaluable lessons about patience, growth, and human potential.

Let us take another interesting example. I give you the following offers—

A. Take ₹20 crores in cash right now

           or

B. Get ₹1 today, ₹2 tomorrow, ₹4 the next day, ₹8 on the fourth day, and so on.

You can choose either A or B, but not both. Many participants in my seminar choose option A. However, offer A gives you only ₹20 crores.

Now, guess how much you would receive if you chose offer B? It would be a whopping amount of more than ₹50 crores. (Try calculating this—it is not difficult.) The power of compounding is simply mind-blowing.

Compounding interest is often referred to as Einstein's eighth wonder of the world. Einstein reportedly said, "The eighth wonder of the world is interest that grows over time. Those who understand it, earn it; those who don't, pay it." At first glance, this quote might seem like a bit of an exaggeration, but the math behind it proves that it's not.

It may sound crazy, but here's what you need to know: Interest that compounds over time has a huge effect on how much money you have later in life. This is why it's crucial to start saving as early as possible. Younger people have a distinct advantage over older ones because they have more time to get the most out of compounding. With a steady income, discipline, and smart investments, you can build a substantial retirement fund so that you can enjoy the life you want.

DO NOT COMPOUND YOUR DEBTS

If you have taken loans and are paying interest, you might become a victim of compounding in a negative manner. For instance, if you have to pay interest at 12% per annum via a bullet payment at the end of six years, the outstanding debt in your account will be double at the end of six years.

Credit card loans are the riskiest as the interest rates charged on credit cards are extremely high. For detailed discussion on this, refer to Chapter 3—*Do Not Fall into a Debt Trap.*

FORMULA TO CALCULATE COMPOUND INTEREST

Although a bit technical, compound interest can be calculated using the following formula:

M = P [1+ (1/N)] NT

Here,   M = Maturity amount

P = Principal

I = Rate of interest

T = Time period

N = Number of periods

While you can calculate compound interest manually using the above formula, it is recommended that you use a compound interest formula calculator to ensure accurate results and avoid errors. Even banks routinely use daily compound interest calculators for this purpose.

BENEFITS OF STARTING EARLY

The following tables illustrate how much you would need to save per month if your savings grow at a rate of 12% compounded annually. We assume that the corpus you will need at the age of 60 is ₹5 crores.

AGE AT THE BEGINNING	INVESTMENT REQUIRED PER MONTH (IN ₹)
20 years	4,208
30 years	14,165
40 years	50,043
50 years	2,15,203

The idea is that anybody in his twenties can easily earn an extra amount of ₹5,000 per month and the same if invested properly may create a mammoth retirement corpus. Refer the section on multiple sources of income to earn additional income.

Let's take the example of American investor and billionaire Warren Buffett. His age-wise approximate net worth is as follows:

At the age of 21	$ 20,000
At the age of 30	$ 1 million
At the age of 39	$ 25 million
At the age of 50	$ 376 million
At the age of 56	$ 1 billion
At the age of 66	$ 17 billion
At the age of 91	$ 117 billion

Buffett has mentioned several times that his immense wealth can be attributed to the power of compounding. The period of investing is equally important—He began investing when he was probably only 10 years old.

I recently read about how each cell in our body starts as a single cell. After the first division, there are two cells. The second time around, there are four, and so on. By the 50th division, our bodies have 1,00,000 billion cells, which is where the process stops. Scientists still don't understand how a single cell can divide into so many different types of cells that can then organize themselves into complex structures like the stomach, brain, skin, teeth, and many other highly specialized parts of the body. Similarly, when money is invested and saved, it can grow at a rate that seems impossible.

It is not necessary to have the goal of earning the highest returns in order to be successful in investing. This is because the highest returns tend to be one-time hits that may not be replicated. Earning returns that are satisfactory enough to maintain and that can be repeated over the longest possible period of time are of utmost importance. When this happens, compounding can become quite chaotic.

POWER OF COMPOUNDING

In compounding, the growth may not be visible initially, but it accelerates exponentially over time. Let's take a simple example: an investment of ₹5,00,000, if invested at 12% per annum, would grow up to ₹10,00,000 in six years. However, it will grow into ₹15,00,000 in the next four years (i.e., in the 10th year from your initial investment). To estimate when your income will approximately be double, triple or quadruple, you can also use the simple Rule of 72, Rule of 114, and Rule of 144.

Rule of 72

- It gives an approximate time it will take to double your money based on the rate of return.

- So, if you earn 12% p.a., then divide 72 by 12. Now, 72/12 = 6.

- Therefore, you will double your investment in six years.

Rule of 114

- It calculates how long it will take for an investment to triple in value based on the rate of return.

- So, if you earn 12% p.a., then divide 114 by 12. Now 114/12 = 9.5.

- Therefore, you will triple your investment in approximately nine years and six months.

Rule of 144

- It calculates how long it will take for an investment to quadruple (i.e., increase fourfold) in value based on the rate of return.

- So, if you earn 12% p.a., then divide 144 by 12. Now 144/2 = 12.

- Therefore, you will quadruple your investment in 12 years.

OTHER USES OF THE ABOVE RULES:

These rules can also be applied to estimate the effect of inflation on your investment. For e.g., ₹10,000 in your hand today is not equal to 10,000 after six or seven years due to inflation. Suppose you invest an amount of ₹10,000 today; its real value after 12 years will be ₹5,000.

To calculate the number of years in which the money will be reduced to 50% if the rate of inflation is 6% per annum, divide 72 by 6, i.e., 72/6= 12. This means that in 12 years, the amount invested will be halved in real value.

The takeaway from here is that *you must earn more than the inflation rate if you want your money to grow.*

This rule can be used in determining when our population will double. For example, if our population is growing 3% per annum, then the population will be double in 24 years (72/3=24).

Similarly, you can estimate how our economy will grow: For example, if our GDP at the moment is growing at the rate of 6%, then our economy size will be doubled in 12 years (72/6=12).

See the following table for more clarity:

PARTICULARS	AMOUNT IN ₹
Initial one-time investment at 12% p.a.	5,00,000
Double in six years	10,00,000
Triple in nine years and six months	15,00,000
Quadruple, i.e., four times in 12 years	20,00,000
Eight times in 18 years	40,00,000
Sixteen times in 24 years	80,00,000
Thirty-two times in 30 years	1,60,00,000

Please note:

1. In the above example, there is only one-time investment of ₹5,00,000.

2. The formula gives an approximate return, not an exact one.

3. The examples provided are intended to help you understand the concept of compounding. To double your money, you must implement most of the lessons mentioned in this book.

There is no shortcut to double your money. As American vaudeville performer and actor, Will Rogers once said: "The quickest way to double your money is to fold it in half and put it in your back pocket."

THE IMPACT OF MONTHLY INVESTING

If you invest ₹10,000 every month (e.g., through a Systematic Investment Plan), your total investment per annum will be ₹1,20,000. Over 30 years, you would have invested ₹36,00,000. However, if you earn a return of 12% p.a., due to the compounding effect, your investment will grow to a colossal amount of ₹3.53 crores.

See the following table:

NO. OF YEARS	PRINCIPAL INVESTMENT	TOTAL INVESTMENT + INTEREST
1	1,20,000	1,28,093
2	2,40,000	2,72,432
3	3,60,000	4,35,076
4	4,80,000	6,18,348
5	6,00,000	8,24,864
10	12,00,000	23,23,391
20	24,00,000	99,91,479
30	36,00,000	3,52,99,138

In the same example, if you top up your investment by 10% (i.e., you invest ₹11,000 in the second year, ₹12,100 in the third, and so on), your investment will grow further, assuming an average rate of return of 12% per annum.

NO. OF YEARS	PRINCIPAL INVESTMENT	TOTAL INVESTMENT + INTEREST
1	1,20,000	1,28,093
2	2,52,000	2,76,339
3	3,97,200	4,56,585
4	5,56,920	6,74,212
5	7,32,612	9,35,411
10	19,12,491	31,84,832
20	68,73,000	1,87,10,327
30	1,97,39,283	8,30,17,801

While most people know the power of compounding, only a few implement it consistently. The time required to see significant results is too long; so patience and discipline are key. Many of my clients would say that life does not run on any mathematical formula; it's a roller coaster ride full of ups and downs. They believe it is not possible to commit for such a long period of time to truly benefit from compounding. I understand their concerns, but let me emphasize that proper planning and strategy are required to face these challenges. The program I have suggested in Chapter 12—*Enjoy Golden Years of Your Life*—will ensure that you can face any hurdle confidently.

Benjamin Franklin rightly said, "Failure to plan is planning to fail." You must be creative while planning to reduce the risk of uncertainty. It is essential to find ways to deal with unexpected incidents.

> *"When it comes to compounding, don't trust your intuition. You have no idea how powerful it is."*
>
> —Manoj Arora, author of From the *Rat Race to Financial Freedom*

CHAPTER 7

COUNT YOUR CASH AND LEAVE THE REST

"There are three faithful friends—an old wife, an old dog, and ready money."

—Benjamin Franklin, American statesman

Every individual, whether in business, profession, or a job, must maintain enough liquidity to fulfill all financial commitments on time. Cash on hand is useful when you spot an opportunity to take benefit of a bargain or a not-to-be-missed offer. There are better solutions to liquidity issues than taking out one loan after another. You must systematically manage your finances by preparing a cash flow statement.

IMPORTANCE OF CASH FLOW STATEMENTS (CFS)

In this chapter, we will explore the importance of cash flow statements (CFS) and how to prepare, manage, and monitor them.

Proper and systematic cash flow management will help you in following ways:

1. You will know your exact liquidity position, which helps plan future operations, investments, and debt reduction to ensure lower interest costs and more profitability.

2. Ensuring timely payments to employees and suppliers that will keep them motivated.

3. It helps identify pain points in your life or business so that immediate corrective action can be taken.

4. When you approach your bankers to fund expansion plans, they will see how much cash your business generates rather than its profitability. It is well-known that an entity with good cash flow enjoys a better valuation.

5. It is essential to prepare your budget monthly, quarterly, or yearly. Cash flow statements help in preparing budgets.

6. Cash flow statements help you plan your savings and retirement corpus by eliminating uncertainties and estimates. Knowing the gap between income and expenditure allows you to plan for specific long-term expenses like vacations, vehicles, houses, weddings, or education. Remember, what you measure improves.

7. Everybody prepares a balance sheet and profit and loss account, but to understand the actual position of the organization or even an individual, you need to study the cash flow statement. This crucial statement guides us in understanding whether a cash surplus (or deficit) is due to improvement in your day-to-day business operations or other reasons like the sale of assets. At the same time, negative

cash flow does not necessarily indicate financial trouble. It may be because the entity has repaid loans or made large capital expenditures. However, the goal over time should be to achieve positive cash flow, where cash inflow exceeds cash outflow. If the financial statements (i.e., balance sheet and profit and loss account) and cash flow statement reflect a similar picture, the stakeholders will have more confidence in such organizations.

8. Ready cash brings opportunities, and you can benefit from them when they appear. You can invest in good bargains and make more money. But most importantly, cash comes in handy during emergencies, for example, in a situation like the COVID-19 pandemic, a layoff, or a setback in business.

9. A healthy liquidity position boosts your confidence. You exude positive energy. Your focus is on growth, development, and earning more money. You become the favourite of your vendors, employees, bankers, and family members.

10. A cash flow statement helps identify cash generation from operating, investing, or financing activities.

So, cash flow statements indicate the real financial health of an organization or individual. Some authors say that the financial statement is fiction and that the cash flow statement is a reality. It is also said that profit is an opinion, but cash flow is the truth. This is because a financial statement only shows a firm's income and expenses but does not reveal how much cash was generated, spent, and invested. Only the cash flow statement provides an insight into a firm's liquidity, ability to generate cash, and evaluation of its financial health and potential for future expansion.

ACCOUNTING IS THE LANGUAGE OF BUSINESS

"A man with a comprehensive background of accounts could not be cheated in business."
—Marianne Bertrand (Belgian economist) and Antoinette Schoar (German-American economist)

If you are running your own business or are self-employed, always pay attention to the importance of proper and timely accounting. Keep your books updated concurrently and reconciled every month.

In my practice, I have observed almost every owner grumbling: "I can't see the profit," "Where has my profit gone?", or "Whether I am making a profit?". A few steps based on my experience might address these issues:

1. Insist on monthly reports from your accountant. Design a format that serves your purpose.

2. Insist on a monthly cash flow statement in addition to profit and loss account and balance sheet.

3. Do not mix personal accounts with business accounts. Maintain them separately.

4. As far as possible, settle suppliers' accounts bill-wise (maybe in two or more tranches). Never make a payment without an invoice.

5. From your cash flow statements, assess whether any short-term or working capital loan has been used for acquiring long-term assets. Correct this as soon as possible. For example, buying an asset like a computer, vehicle, or machinery using

cash credit limit is a bad idea. You should take a term loan or ensure sufficient cash surplus for this specific purpose.

6. Never assume that your profit equals your cash inflow. For example, the books might reflect a profit of ₹50 lakhs, yet the cash flow may be negative. Cash is king, not profit. Find out the reasons for negative cash flow despite huge profits. The following are the probable reasons:

    a) Disproportionate increase in outstanding debtors.

    b) Increase in inventories.

    c) Withdrawals by the owner.

    d) Short-term funds used for long-term purposes.

    e) Malpractices in the firm.

    f) Disproportionate increase in expenses.

    g) Seasonal businesses, like coaching classes, might face some cash crunches in non-seasonal months.

    h) Increase in bad and doubtful debts.

    i) No growth in sales.

7. If you have more than one product or service, determine the profitability of each one of them. This is known as segment accounting, which enables you to decide which segment to focus on. The idea is that there is no point in carrying a continuous loss-making unit. There might be some exceptions, such as the property you hold for this loss-making business is increasing in value by leaps and bounds.

8. Remember that every penny is important, and a rupee saved is a rupee earned. Always maintain a sweep-in or flexi deposit account so that you earn interest on surplus liquidity. For

example, if you have to pay GST on the 20th of December for the transaction that occurred during November, you can earn some interest for the intervening period.

9.   Maintain proper co-ordination with your accountant and their team. You must regularly interact with the accounts team, understand their problems, and give them the support they need. Remember, every transaction the accountant records has financial implications. If proper inputs are not provided, the accountant will be helpless.

For example, you cannot blame the accountant if there is a severe liquidity problem and an EMI bounces. However, at the same time, the accountant is duty-bound to inform the owner well in advance that the EMI will hit on a specific date. They might give valuable suggestions like stepping up the recovery procedure, optimizing inventory level, and generating funds creatively. The accountant can advise the owner to set daily, weekly, fortnightly, and monthly targets for the person responsible for recovery.

Another critical piece of advice is to maintain a cushion or emergency fund equivalent to three months of urgent outflows, such as EMIs, electricity, salaries, wages, etc. Similarly, making a budget or projected cash flow is equally important.

10. Before firing your accountant, review the culture prevailing in your organization. Firing and hiring seldom resolve the issues. It is found that tiredness is the main reason accountants do not perform their job at optimum level and ultimately quit. Non-supporting culture, extended working hours, related stress, shortages, and inefficiencies at the

grassroots level result in mental and physical exhaustion. Every employee nowadays is looking for a work-life balance.

According to a survey by the American Institute of Certified Public Accountants (AICPA), burnout is one of the reasons accountants quit their jobs. Long hours, high stress levels, and heavy workloads lead to burnout and physical and mental exhaustion.

Therefore, unless you identify the root cause, simply firing and hiring will prove to be a futile exercise. Whenever I visit one of my clients, I find the owner interviewing new candidates. Firing and hiring have become a norm in his organization. And believe me, this pattern has continued for decades. Some people are not coachable.

11. Organize your accounts department so that it can produce results and submit timely reports to the owner. Setting up an accounts department in a small organization is not rocket science. Consider the below given flowchart:

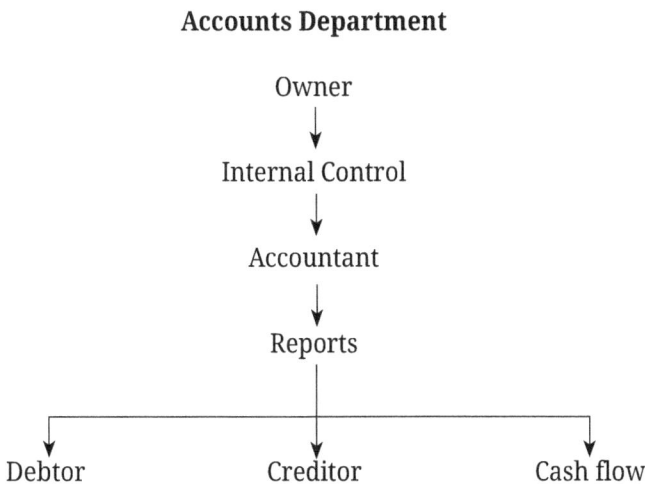

Accounts Department

Owner
↓
Internal Control
↓
Accountant
↓
Reports

Debtor   Creditor   Cash flow

Larger organizations may have more layers depending on volume, need, and convenience. Reports generated by the accounts departments must be discussed with the owner weekly, fortnightly, or monthly. Action points emerging from the discussion should be implemented diligently with proper follow-through in the next meeting. Let this practice become a habit.

I have observed that many clients depend on bank SMS alerts to know their bank balance. This is a bad practice. Always ensure that the accountant provides an up-to-date bank ledger with accurate bank balance figures. Sometimes, due to technical issues, we do not receive SMS alerts from banks. Therefore, as a matter of habit, always rely on the up-to-date bank passbook in the accounting software system. One of my clients adopted a policy that the accountant's mobile number was shared with the bank. This puts additional accountability on the accountant to maintain complete records and present a correct picture to the owner.

12. We know that our expenses should be less than our income to maintain a certain financial discipline. Similarly, barring exceptional cases, our cash outflow must be less than our cash inflow.

13. Do not let the paucity of time with the accountant become an excuse to avoid or delay the preparation of the cash flow statement. Generally, an accountant is engaged in his real work for less than 60% of the day. Work expands as per availability of time.

I advise one exercise to ensure proper time management for any individual. Write down the work done every hour. The format may be like this:

TIME (12-HOUR CLOCK)	ACTIVITIES
10.00 a.m. to 11.00 a.m.	
11.00 a.m. to 12.00 p.m.	
12.00 p.m. to 01.00 p.m.	
01.00 p.m. to 02.00 p.m.	
02.00 p.m. to 03.00 p.m.	
03.00 p.m. to 04.00 p.m.	
04.00 p.m. to 05.00 p.m.	
05.00 p.m. to 06.00 p.m.	
06.00 p.m. to 07.00 p.m.	

If the above chart is prepared for one week, you will be surprised to see how many unproductive hours you have. This eye-opening exercise will significantly improve the output of employees.

PREPARE YOUR OWN CASH FLOW STATEMENT

Preparing the cash flow statement is simple, and anyone, even the ones without a finance background, can do it. All it requires is to collate all your receipts and all your payments, however small they may be. Once you start preparing it, it will become a habit, and your quarterly cash flow statement will be ready in less than 60 minutes.

See the following example carefully. You may use a journal or an Excel sheet as per your preference.

Cash Flow Statement
(For Individual)

DESCRIPTION	APRIL TO JUNE	JULY TO SEPTEMBER	OCTOBER TO DECEMBER	JANUARY TO MARCH
Opening balance				
(except Emergency Reserve) (1)				
Net active income (2)				
Other incomes (3)				
Loans				
1) Home Loan				
2) Credit cards				
3) Others				
Total (A)				
Investments				
1) SIP				
2) Specific purpose funds				
3) Other funds				
Household expenses				

DESCRIPTION	APRIL TO JUNE	JULY TO SEPTEMBER	OCTOBER TO DECEMBER	JANUARY TO MARCH
Other expenses (be specific)				
Rent or EMI				
Others				
Emergencies				
Insurance				
Total (B)				
Closing balance (A-B)				

Notes:

1. Your emergency reserve is not included in the opening cash balance, as these reserves are used only in case of extreme exigency.

2. Net active income refers to net take-home income. It is net of taxes and other deductions like EPF.

3. Other incomes include all incomes other than active income, such as dividends, interest, rent, royalty, and income from part-time pursuits.

4. Specific purpose funds are categories of investment that include savings that you accumulate for short-term or medium-term purposes, such as vacations, weddings, education, vehicles, etc.

5. The closing balance at the end of the quarter becomes the opening balance of the next quarter.

ANALYZE YOUR CASH FLOW STATEMENT

Once you have prepared your cash flow statement, you must analyze the same to identify those areas which need improvement. Here are a few suggestions:

- If your cash balance is consistently high, consider investing or reducing debts

- Your annual income must grow to beat inflation. For this purpose, compare the cash flow statement over two years

- Similarly, your income from non-active sources or passive income should show an upward trend. Ensure that your contributions towards investments match your income

- If your essential and non-essential expenses are increasing disproportionately, analyze them by categorizing them under 'needs' and 'wants' as discussed in Chapter 5 *Expenses Matter*

- Loans taken should be reduced gradually by prioritizing those with highest interest rates. Credit card outstandings should be brought to zero at the earliest

- Monitor your specific purpose funds closely. For example, if you plan to buy a car after three years, ensure to maintain sufficient balance in this fund to purchase the car without or with a minimum loan

- Always make sufficient provisions to pay insurance premiums and taxes on time

- If cash inflow is less than the previous quarter, determine the reason for the same and take appropriate corrective measures. Knowledge is bliss; ignorance is not

- Feel free to modify the cash flow statement to suit your specific needs and circumstances

The above-mentioned cash flow statement has been explained keeping an individual in mind. To learn how to prepare a cash flow statement for proprietorship concerns and small firms, visit: www.indiagrowthacademy.com

"Revenue is vanity, profit is sanity, and cash is king."

—Alan Miltz, Co-founder Cash Flow Story

CHAPTER 8

TRACK YOUR WEALTH

"If you can't measure it, you can't manage it."
—Peter Drucker, Austrian-American consultant
and educator

In this chapter, we are not talking about your income. We are talking about your wealth—your net worth. Income is not wealth; your net worth definitely is. We pay income tax on income, but in India, we do not pay any tax on wealth.

Income is what you earn, and wealth is what you keep. So, two tenets of being wealthy are: *earn more* and *spend less*. How much you must earn to become wealthy? It is quite subjective. One may think a person earning ₹1 lakh per month is rich, while someone earning ₹50,000 isn't. But what if a person earning ₹1 lakh spends ₹1,25,000 (*"Credit cards hain na*! – We can always rely on credit cards!") and a person earning ₹50,000 spends only ₹30,000? It's not about earning; it's about how much you save and invest.

In other words, what gets measured can also be controlled. Unfortunately, many do not know our real net worth, income, expenses, and savings. We act on an ad-hoc basis, spending impulsively. Saving then becomes an accident, not a routine. You may still go wrong despite all your planning, but it is better to be alert and aware of whatever is happening. That is the only way to mitigate turbulences and upheavals.

In calculating your net worth, keep the following points in mind:

WHAT IS NET WORTH?

As per *Investopedia*, net worth is the difference between what you *own* and what you *owe*. If your assets exceed your liabilities, you have a positive net worth. Conversely, if your liabilities exceed your assets, your net worth is negative. Net worth is also called net wealth. Knowing your net wealth makes it easier to set your goal. The problem is that many of us do not know our real net worth. Calculating one's net worth takes effort, which most of us avoid. Net worth is nothing but a number that reveals the value of the assets you own, minus your liabilities.

Your net worth statement is a barometer to determine your assets, debts, and other liabilities on a particular date. If your net worth on March 31, 2022 was ₹150 lakhs and on March 31, 2023, ₹165 lakhs, you know that during the preceding year, your net worth has gone up by ₹15 lakhs. In other words, it has increased by 10%. Your target is to ensure that there is positive growth. You compete with yourself, not with others. A negative growth will instantly alert you that your finances are going wrong. You can monitor your debts and your final goal to live a debt-free life. Your net worth number plays an important role in asset allocation, i.e., diversifying your assets into different classes. For example, if you have a home loan, you may like to keep it at 40% of your net worth.

As mentioned in an earlier chapter, we discussed the significance of specific purpose funds for various expenses, such as buying a house, a car, going on vacation, weddings, and education, etc. A net worth statement will guide you properly when you incur a large expense. You might like to wait for a few years before buying a car or your dream house. In short, net worth statements are instrumental in realizing your financial goals and ultimately enjoying financial freedom.

HOW OFTEN YOU SHOULD CHECK NET WORTH?

You can track your net worth more often (or less) than every quarter. Some prefer monthly charts, while some prefer half-yearly tracking. There is no hard and fast rule. Follow what suits you.

KEEP IT CONFIDENTIAL

If you maintain the net worth tracker on an Excel sheet, you may take a printout every quarter and file it safely or save it on your mobile. Since it is generally a single-page statement, one of my clients keeps it in his purse. Keep it in a place where you might see it occasionally, but at the same time, ensure that others cannot access it. It's your "confidential" statement. Earlier, I was using the INDmoney app, but now I maintain it in an Excel sheet. When you fill in the figures every quarter, it triggers an emotion response that pushes you to achieve your target. You are motivated to perform a specific milestone or objective. These emotional responses make you wise. Even if circumstances are unfavorable, it alerts you and your surroundings to take appropriate action. It reminds you of your goal, your commitment, and the skills you must develop.

Another reason I track my net worth in an Excel spreadsheet is that I want all my data on my laptop, and it does not take more than 30 minutes every quarter. Excel sheets are more reliable and trusted, providing enough flexibility to customize and control my net worth. However, tech-savvy readers can use appropriate software or apps to minimize the labour of manual input.

APPROXIMATE MARKET VALUE IS SUFFICIENT

Where the exact market value is not available, take the approximate value. Your net worth statement need not reflect 100% of market value; about 90% accuracy is a good enough score. But in any case, maintain consistency and follow the same rule every quarter.

Remember, the purpose of tracking net worth is to help you achieve financial goals. So be realistic and include only those assets that can be liquidated and converted into money. Take, for example, a car you own. It's a depreciating asset, so you must take the depreciated value of your car. Every quarter, the car's value will decrease by 3% to 4%. Similarly, do not include assets that cannot be easily converted into money, such as furniture, TVs, kitchen equipment, washing machine, etc.

IS YOUR HOUSE AN ASSET?

The vast majority of people do not sell their house except in three cases:

- To buy a bigger house
- A change in location of job, business, etc.
- In case of extreme financial difficulties to avoid bankruptcy

Remember, I previously advised you to not take a housing loan of more than 60% of the value of your primary residence. So, if you consider only 50% of the value of your residence in your net worth, you provide enough cushion against future uncertainties while keeping yourself motivated. In any case, there is no harm in this approach, as, at the back of your mind, you always know the true market value of your property.

HIGH NET WORTH INDIVIDUALS (HNI)

An HNI is an individual who has substantial net wealth. There is no fixed rule as to the threshold for qualifying as an HNI, but generally, an individual with over ₹5 crores in net worth may be considered an HNI.

Now the question arises: if you have a residential house that is more than ₹5 crores, will you be considered an HNI? The answer is *no* unless you have other investible assets worth more than ₹5 crores. So, your primary residence and other assets that cannot be liquidated are generally excluded from the net worth. However, when calculating your net worth, we consider all your assets and all your liabilities. A cautious approach is to take only 50% of the value of the primary residence in your net worth.

Recently, one of my clients sold his primary residence in south Mumbai and purchased another one in the central suburb, costing him only 50% of the amount realized on the existing residence. There is no hard and fast rule. Once you are aware of the method you choose, it's perfectly alright.

If your net worth is around ₹1.5 crores, according to Knight Frank— the global real estate agency—you are among the top 1% of wealthy people in India. So, if you're not following this practice of tracking your net worth, I suggest you start with it right away as it might give you a much-needed motivation.

NET WORTH CHART HAS ITS OWN LIMITATIONS

A net worth chart must be used only for tracking your growth. It does not guarantee that you are leading a good life. Poor liquidity and many debts will make one's life miserable despite having a crore in net worth. So, for a comfortable life, your income should be more than your expenses, and your net worth should be positive.

DO NOT WORRY IF YOUR NET WORTH GOES DOWN TEMPORARILY

Temporary fluctuation in net worth is not a major cause for concern. It is the overall trend that is important. It is okay if your net worth grows at a reasonable compounding rate of return in the long run. However, the continuous decline in the value of any particular asset class must be looked into. For example, if the return from a mutual fund investment is below expectations, seek some professional advice and reshuffle the portfolio.

YOUR IDEAL NET WORTH

What should be your ideal net worth? A rough rule to calculate ideal net worth (i.e., minimum net worth) is to divide a person's age by 10 and then multiply it by their gross annual income.

Suppose Mr. Ronit is 50 years old. His gross total income per annum is ₹30 lakhs. His ideal net worth should be (50/10) x 30 = ₹150 lakhs.

Another rule says your net worth by the age of 40 must be twice your annual gross total income and the same should increase by one point every five years.

So, if Mr. Ronit is 40 years old and his salary or gross total income is ₹30 lakhs, and presuming about 10% growth in annual income, his net worth at different stages of life should be:

AGE (IN YEARS)	ANNUAL INCOME X (MULTIPLICATION FACTOR)	NET WORTH REQUIRED (IN ₹)
40	30 x 2	60 lakhs
45	33 x 3	99 lakhs
50	36 x 4	144 lakhs
55	40 x 5	200 lakhs
60	44 x 6	264 lakhs
65	49 x 7	343 lakhs
70	54 x 8	432 lakhs

NET WORTH STATEMENT TO BE READ ALONG WITH CASH FLOW STATEMENT

Your net worth combined with a cash flow statement helps you determine the amount of spending, saving, withdrawals, and accumulation of wealth to achieve the goal of financial freedom.

You must know your liquidity position to commit to further investments. Similarly, if cash inflow is negative, you might have to liquidate some of your investments in certain situations. So, be practical. Be modest and realistic, but never kill your dreams.

NEGATIVE NET WORTH

Negative net worth means your liabilities exceed your assets. It's an alarming situation. Please go through the Chapter 3—*Do Not Fall into a Debt Trap*—once again and take immediate action. High levels of debts, mortgages, credit card outstandings, etc., are the main reasons behind negative net worth. Many times, negative net worth is due to overspending and poor saving habits. Sometimes it may be due to genuine emergencies like huge medical bills, business losses, litigation, fraud, etc. Check your pattern and work on it before it is too late.

The net worth chart may also assist you in the following ways:

- It comes in handy in case you want to raise loans from financial institutions
- You can monitor growth (or otherwise) in your net worth
- You may set goals for the future
- It helps you diversify your portfolio
- It keeps you motivated to save more, invest more, and spend less. Your confidence level increases as you know you are moving in the right direction
- It helps in determining the insurance cover for your assets
- You know at a glance whether you are prepared to handle any unforeseen disaster. Never think that disaster happens only to others
- If you share the net worth statement with your close family members, it helps in smooth planning of succession
- You know which investments are doing well and which aren't

Below is a model net worth tracking table. This is not exhaustive; it's indicative. Not everyone has similar assets; not everyone has the same liabilities. You know better what your assets and liabilities are.

WHAT IS MY CAPITAL NET WORTH?

Name:

Low-Risk Assets (A)

PARTICULARS	QUARTER ENDED JUNE 30	QUARTER ENDED SEPT. 30	QUARTER ENDED DEC. 31	QUARTER ENDED MARCH 31
Liquid assets				
Cash balance				
Bank balance				
Fixed deposits				
Government bonds				
Sovereign gold bonds				
Loans to friends/ relatives				
Debt funds				
Mutual funds (short-term)				

PARTICULARS	QUARTER ENDED JUNE 30	QUARTER ENDED SEPT. 30	QUARTER ENDED DEC. 31	QUARTER ENDED MARCH 31
Provident funds				
NPS				
Precious metals				
Gratuity				
Deposits with government bodies				
Total of Low-Risk Assets (A)				

Medium-Risk Assets (B)

PARTICULARS	QUARTER ENDED JUNE 30	QUARTER ENDED SEPT. 30	QUARTER ENDED DEC. 31	QUARTER ENDED MARCH 31
Mutual funds				
Listed equities				
Capital investments in partnership firms				
Insurance policies (cash value)				

PARTICULARS	QUARTER ENDED JUNE 30	QUARTER ENDED SEPT. 30	QUARTER ENDED DEC. 31	QUARTER ENDED MARCH 31
Self-occupied residential properties (50% of market value)				
Other real estate assets				
Vehicles (depreciated value)				
Others				
Total of Medium-Risk Assets (B)				

High-Risk Assets

PARTICULARS	QUARTER ENDED JUNE 30	QUARTER ENDED SEPT. 30	QUARTER ENDED DEC. 31	QUARTER ENDED MARCH 31
Corporate bonds				
ESOPs				
Unlisted equities				
Arts and collectibles				

PARTICULARS	QUARTER ENDED JUNE 30	QUARTER ENDED SEPT. 30	QUARTER ENDED DEC. 31	QUARTER ENDED MARCH 31
Loans to non-relatives				
Profit-sharing ventures				
Receivables				
Bitcoins				
Others				
Total of Medium-Risk Assets (C)				
TOTAL ASSETS (A+B+C) = D				

Liabilities

PARTICULARS	QUARTER ENDED JUNE 30	QUARTER ENDED SEPT. 30	QUARTER ENDED DEC. 31	QUARTER ENDED MARCH 31
Long-term liabilities (E)				
Housing loans				
Other mortgages				
Car loans				

PARTICULARS	QUARTER ENDED JUNE 30	QUARTER ENDED SEPT. 30	QUARTER ENDED DEC. 31	QUARTER ENDED MARCH 31
Others				
Total long-term liabilities (E)				

Short-term Liabilities (F)

PARTICULARS	QUARTER ENDED JUNE 30	QUARTER ENDED SEPT. 30	QUARTER ENDED DEC. 31	QUARTER ENDED MARCH 31
Personal loans				
Overdrafts				
Friendly loans				
Credit card outstandings				
Unpaid bills				
Income tax				
Commitment to NGOs				
Payables				
Others				
Total short-term liabilities (F)				

PARTICULARS	QUARTER ENDED JUNE 30	QUARTER ENDED SEPT. 30	QUARTER ENDED DEC. 31	QUARTER ENDED MARCH 31
Total liabilities (E+F)= G				
Net worth (D-G)				
% of growth over the previous quarter /year				

Tracking your net worth is an important step towards your journey to financial freedom. This is the barometer that determines the wheels of your financial life.

You start from your current net worth and watch it grow quarter after quarter. The art is not in making money and buying assets but in maintaining and growing them. Discipline and responsible action are the keys to your financial freedom.

"Financial stability is much more about doing the best with what you have and not about achieving a certain level of income."
—Erik Wecks, Author of *How to Manage Your Money When You Don't Have Any*

CHAPTER 9

PROTECT YOUR ASSETS THROUGH DIVERSIFICATION

"Put all your eggs in one basket, and then watch that basket."[19]
—Andrew Carnegie, Scottish-American industrialist
and philanthropist

WHAT IS DIVERSIFICATION?

Diversifying your portfolio to ensure a reasonable return on investment while greatly mitigating risk is essential. As a prudent investor, your primary goal should be to reduce portfolio risk. By mixing a wide variety of asset classes in your portfolio, you ensure that even if there is a loss in one asset, the other assets will not be affected. Thus, it is important to choose more than one asset class.

WHAT IS AN ASSET CLASS?

An "asset class" is a collection of investments which are of similar nature and characteristics and are subject to the same risk. An ideal portfolio has a diverse selection of asset classes which are not correlated. Investments in equities, mutual funds, or portfolio management scheme (PMS) are correlated and have same risk. But investment in stocks, gold, and debt funds are not correlated and come under different asset classes. For example, if you invest heavily in real estate spread over different properties, you still carry the same risk if there is a recession in the real estate market, as the 'product' (the real estate) remains the same. Most common examples of asset classes include equities, fixed income, commodities, and real estate.[20] They are comparable with the products in the same asset class but are uncorrelated with other asset classes like stocks and gold.

Diversification or asset allocation plays a vital role in your financial planning. If you wish to invest substantially in different equities and stocks, you must diversify your investments. Therefore, choose the right investment tool within each asset class that aligns with your financial goal. Diversification can occur both within the same asset class and across different asset classes. For example, if you are investing in stocks, you may have the following options:

1. Size of the company, i.e., large-cap, mid-cap, small-cap, micro-cap, etc.

2. Operations beyond local jurisdictions.

3. Sector-wise investment, such as banking, manufacturing, pharma, etc.

4. Overseas companies, i.e., investing in different regions.

5. Payout considerations, such as whether the company is regularly declaring dividends or not.

Investing outside of a particular asset class is equally important. Examples include real estate, debt funds, precious metals, alternative investments, etc. Much depends on your risk appetite, time horizon, financial goal, health status, and your mindset.

The essential rules to be followed are:

1. Don't put all eggs in one basket.
2. Stick to basics.
3. Scale up your investment.

Let's discuss different instruments forming various asset classes:

FIXED DEPOSITS AND BONDS

Indians, by and large, love to have fixed bank deposits because they provide security, liquidity, and regular income. The interest rate is higher in fixed deposits compared to the interest we get in our savings accounts. However, the million-dollar question you must ask is whether you can beat inflation by investing in fixed deposits. The second question is how much should one invest in fixed deposits.

Let me answer the second question first. You should park your emergency fund, reserve fund, and cushion fund in investments like fixed deposits or liquid funds, even though the return is less than other avenues of investments.

However, investing solely on fixed deposits is not a good idea, as its returns are generally lower than the inflation rate. One simple formula every investor must follow is that your return on investment must outpace inflation. If your returns are less than the inflation rate, you will receive a negative return.

Ensure that part of your fixed deposit investments is available in an emergency. Find out good schemes, like a sweep-in facility, but be sure to understand the terms and conditions before investing.

Beware of small cooperative banks that are likely to default. Invest in those banks only to the extent that is covered by deposit insurance, which currently stands at ₹5 lakhs.

Taxation is another aspect you should consider before investing in fixed deposits. Interest earned on FDs is fully taxable unless you are above the age of 60, in which case an amount up to ₹50,000 is exempt under section 80TTB of the Income Tax Act.

Investment in company or government bonds is another way of investing in fixed-income instruments. Deposits with corporates may carry risk depending on the size, track record, net worth, and profitability of the corporations.

MUTUAL FUNDS

"A mutual fund is a financial vehicle that pools assets from shareholders to invest in securities like stocks, bonds, money market instruments, and other assets. Mutual funds are operated by professional money managers who allocate the fund's assets and attempt to produce capital gains or income for the fund's investors. A mutual fund's portfolio is structured and maintained to match the investment objectives stated in its prospectus."[21]

Considered safe in the long run and as one of the most popular investment vehicles, a mutual fund is a pool of money managed by an expert. A mutual fund acts like a trust that collects money from a large number of investors and then invests it in stocks, bonds, and other securities as per the objective of the mutual fund. Because these investments are diversified and well-researched, the chances of suffering losses due to dismal performance of any particular asset are greatly reduced.

Mutual funds may be a good starting point for investors who are new to the stock market, and the earlier you start, the better off you will be. Mutual funds offer three key facilities:

Systematic Investment Plan (SIP): This feature allows investors to invest a set amount at regular intervals into a certain fund.

Systematic Transfer Plan (STP): A facility that allows an investor to move a fixed amount at predetermined intervals from one scheme to another.

Systematic Withdrawal Plan (SWP): This allows you to withdraw a fixed amount from an existing mutual fund at a predetermined interval.

Mutual funds can offer you one of the best and most effective solutions for retirement planning. The SIP investment mode enables you to contribute smaller but consistent amounts, with or without top-up, giving you the advantage of cost averaging, which, in turn, takes care of market volatility.

Essentially, SIP lets an investor accumulate wealth until retirement. After that, a strategic investment management process for withdrawals can yield the desired returns.

INVEST IN EQUITY THROUGH SIP

When you start early, age is on your side, and you likely have a higher risk appetite. Thus, a significant presence in equity through diversified equity funds is recommended. SIP should be your priority to ensure systematic investments. To put things in perspective, if you start a monthly SIP of ₹5,000 at the age of 25, you will place an overall deposit of ₹21 lakhs till you retire in 35 years. Considering a long-term average CAGR (Compound annual growth rate) of 15%, your total investment value could grow to ₹5.7 crores. This is the power of compounding, but the downside is that returns are not guaranteed.

CONSIDER SIP TOP-UP

Adding a minimum 5% top-up to your SIP ensures your monthly investment grows yearly as your salary or income increases. For instance, applying this feature on an SIP worth ₹5,000 would help you accumulate wealth worth ₹8.2 crores in 35 years. A 10% top-up, which is highly recommended, could result in a staggering ₹13.63 crores by the time you retire.

STOP SIP AND SWITCH AT 60

Upon retirement, it is advisable to stop SIP and switch investments to the Balanced Advantage Fund (BAF). This strategy will help conserve and grow your portfolio while providing reasonably good returns.

WITHDRAW SYSTEMATICALLY

Often, investors make the mistake of redeeming the whole of their accumulated corpus in one go. Instead, consider using features like SWP, which allows you to withdraw the required sum monthly by selling a proportionate number of units while the remaining investments continue to grow in value. Let's assume you would need ₹3 lakhs for your monthly expenses post your retirement. On a ₹5.7 crores accumulated corpus parked in BAF, initiating SWP with a 5% top-up can effectively serve you for the next 20 years with a 5% additional sum every year. Interestingly, even when you are 80, you could still have a balance of ₹7.4 crores, assuming a 10% CAGR in BAF.

Mutual funds purchased through a broking firm have higher AMC (Annual Maintenance Charges), so buying directly from the fund house—where you get the fund at Direct NAV (Net Asset Value)—is advisable. As a result, over many years, this will give you a better return (every penny saved is a penny earned).

You need money, strategy, and time—factors you ought to carefully consider. Investing for the long term can significantly improve your returns from mutual funds. By following the 15-15-15 rule, for example, you can build a seven-figure portfolio.

THE 15-15-15 RULE

This rule follows a series of three 15s to help investors achieve seven-figure returns. According to the rule, if you invest ₹15,000 monthly for 15 years in a fund scheme that provides a 15% annual return, you can accumulate ₹1 crore by the end of your tenure. To make this investment, you only need a total investment of ₹27 lakhs, while you will earn ₹73 lakhs. If you extend your investment for another 15 years, your corpus will grow to ₹10 crores, and so on.

EQUITIES

When you invest directly in company stocks, remember the two rules propagated by American investor and businessman Warren Buffet:

Rule No. 1: Never lose your money.

Rule No. 2: Never forget Rule No. 1.

Invest in companies with good track records and that continuously grow in turnover, profitability, and expansion. Never invest based on rumors, tips, or social media news. Do your own research based on above rules. Your stock investments will naturally depend upon your risk appetite and time horizon. One should invest in equities early in life when your risk-taking capacity is higher. As you approach retirement, your equity investment should decrease while your security-oriented investments should go up.

As a thumb rule, one can follow the '100 minus age' formula. For instance, a 25-year-old investor can invest 75% in equities (100-25=75) and the remaining 25% in debt. Some advocate the '110 minus age' rule, but know that these are broad generalizations. They ignore other aspects like time horizon, risk appetite, and expected returns. A 25-year-old investor, for example, might want to retire at 45, while a 45-year-old investor might plan to retire at 70. It is advisable to sync your investments with your goals.

If you plan to buy a car after two or three years, you should invest 100% in debt. How much to invest in equity is highly personalized, and there is no one-size-fits-all solution. Proper diversification and asset allocation are crucial to success. Stock investment is worth it if your time horizon is quite long. It is often said that if you want to save for less than 10 years, do not invest in stocks.

American economist Paul Samuelson rightly says, "Investing should be more like watching paint dry or watching grass grow. If you want excitement, take $800 and go to Las Vegas."

Indian investor Sandeep Sahajpal says, "If you do choose to invest in shares, invest for the lifetime."

It will be a good practice to study the sector in which the company operates and the company's economic behaviour. You can find useful information on various websites, such as:

- www.nseindia.com
- www.bseindia.com
- www.valueresearchonline.com

For beginners, I sincerely advise picking up stocks that declare dividends. Generally, only those companies declare dividend which are doing well and have good profitability. Cash flow is very important, along with capital appreciation. Similarly, large-cap and blue-chip companies are preferred by most of the investors. Risk-takers can opt for mid-cap and small-cap in the hope that they will become blue-chip companies in the future.

GOLD

Gold plays a significant role in asset allocation and diversification of your portfolio. In the good old days, gold was considered merely a backup support in case of emergency or a major event in the family like a wedding. For instance, a client of mine buys gold monthly in small quantities so that after about a decade, it will help in the marriage of his daughter. While gold was not considered a pure investment in the past, times have changed. Today, gold is widely used to diversify the portfolio as it is safe and a good hedge against inflation. Investment in gold during a recession has paid good returns to the investors. Look at the price of gold during the last two decades in the following table:

YEAR	YEARLY AVG. RATE (₹) PER 10 GM (24 CARAT)
2000	4,400
2005	7,000
2010	18,500
2015	26,345
2016	28,623
2017	29,667
2018	31,438
2019	35,220
2020	48,650

YEAR	YEARLY AVG. RATE (₹) PER 10 GM (24 CARAT)
2021	48,720
2022	52,670
2023	65,330
2024	71,500

Thus, gold price has gone up from ₹4,400 in 2000 to over ₹71,000 in 2024. It has grown more than 16 times in about 24 years. The compounded annual growth rate of return over 24 years is 12.32%.

For risk-averse investors, gold investments in India might be the best choice. The fact that gold has no association with other asset classes is by far its biggest advantage. As a result, it can act as a safety net for your portfolio's volatility.

Gold is a finite and naturally occurring resource. Due to increased demand, its market price rises, making gold investment in India a wise choice. Even the strongest currencies may lose value as a result of market uncertainty, but gold, unlike money, is an asset that cannot be produced. As a result, investing in gold in India might shield investors from currency depreciation.

In times of difficulty, gold performs exceptionally well. During a crisis, the stock market typically declines, prompting investors to seek safer investments like gold.

So, how much to invest in gold?

It depends on your asset allocation plan. As a thumb rule, your investment in gold could be anywhere between 5% and 10% of your total portfolio.

Investment in gold need not be in physical form. There are many options available nowadays. The following are a few of them:

i. MUTUAL FUNDS

Some mutual funds include gold in their portfolios. So, by investing in these funds, you invest in gold without physically buying it.

Invesco India Gold Fund, Nippon India Gold Savings Fund, SBI Gold, DSP World Gold Fund, IDBI Gold Fund, Quantum Gold Savings, and Kotak Gold are a few of the gold mutual funds in India.

ii. GOLD EXCHANGE-TRADED FUNDS (ETFS)

Exchange-traded funds have become a convenient way to buy gold. ETFs that invest in gold are essentially tradable funds on stock exchanges. Investors must purchase at least one unit equal to one gram of gold to start trading in gold ETFs. A few of the popular gold ETFs in India include Axis Gold ETFs, Birla Sun Life ETF, UTI Gold Exchange Traded Fund, HDFC Gold Exchange Traded Fund, Invesco Gold Exchange Traded Fund, and Reliance Gold Exchange Traded Fund, among others.

Starting an SIP is another planned way to invest in gold ETFs. Conversion into physical gold is also possible once the investor holds a substantial number of units.

iii. GOLD FUTURE CONTRACTS

Mainly traded in Multi-commodity Exchange (MCX) and National Commodity and Derivatives Exchange Limited (NCDEX), gold futures are highly risky as the investors have to commit to buying gold at an agreed price today, but with a settlement scheduled for a day in the future. In my opinion, this is not for general investors.

iv. SOVEREIGN GOLD BONDS SCHEME (SGB)

In November 2015, the Government of India (GOI) launched the Sovereign Gold Bond Scheme under the Gold Monetization Scheme. In coordination with the GOI, the RBI opened the issues for subscription in tranches under this plan. The RBI regularly announces the scheme's terms and conditions.

SGBs are issued by the RBI and can be purchased by resident Indian entities after completing the KYC process. The bonds are denominated in multiples of one gram of gold and has an eight-year term with exit option available in the fifth, sixth, and seventh year. The compensation for the investors is fixed at 2.5% per annum, payable every six months on the nominal value. All the branches of State Bank of India are authorized to accept the subscription.

REAL ESTATE

"Buy land. They are not making any more."
—Mark Twain, American writer and humourist

Every sensible investor must recognize the potential of investing in real estate. It has become an effective vehicle for wealth creation. The population explosion, gap in demand and supply, and rapid urbanization have fuelled the growth of this sector. This has received further momentum because of funding made available by banks, non-banking finance companies, and other institutions. The real estate sector is well diversified, offering a plethora of options for the investor. Consider the following:

1. Land
2. Housing sector
3. Commercial properties
4. Industrial properties
5. Warehousing
6. Under–construction properties
7. Malls and shopping complex
8. Farm houses
9. Hospitality industry
10. Resorts
11. REITs (Real Estate Investment Trusts)
12. INVITs (Infrastructure Investment Trust)

There are basically two ways of earning money from most of the real estate investments:

• Capital gain
• Rental income

Real estate investments are safe, permanent, and have less volatility, but this is a highly localized sector. The property's price differs from place to place, time to time, and location to location. It lacks liquidity as it cannot be sold as quickly as stocks or gold. Additionally, it has regular maintenance costs like local taxes, repairs, security, insurance, etc.

Real estate appreciation is primarily determined by the property's location, nearby amenities, infrastructure in the area (such as hospitals, schools, malls, and airports), quality of construction, builder reputation, future development of the locality, and so on. Prima facie, the real estate sector appears promising and lucrative. However, it is full of complexities and uncertainties. You need to take extra care before you invest in the real estate sector. Here are a few pointers:

- Analyze your needs and requirements. Whether you are buying a residential property to live in or rent out for passive income?

- Assess your financial resources. If you are buying a property purely as an investment, then you must treat it as a long-term investment

- For passive income, commercial properties may offer better returns. However, this depends on location, accessibility, and many other factors

- Plan ahead. How will you fund the real estate investment? Analyze the cost of bank loans if you plan to go for the same. Cash flow management is crucial in real estate investment; you might suffer a significant loss if you have to sell the property under distress

- If you purchase the property to rent out, consider in advance the impact of EMI, local taxes, maintenance, vacancy, security, etc., where you may have to spend a lot

- Ensure that all documents related to the property are fully legal to avoid potential litigation. Besides the sale deed, you must procure a copy of the building plan, a share certificate from the cooperative society, or a certificate from the builder, housing board, etc. It is advisable to get help from a competent legal professional at the time of purchase. Ensure all requisite approvals have been obtained by the builder or seller. Inspect the property personally before purchase to ensure no part of it is damaged

- If you plan to take a loan against your property, ask yourself: How much can I borrow? Although there is no one-size-fits-all answer, as a general rule, your essential expenses plus all monthly repayment commitments (EMIs, credit card payments, etc.) should not exceed 60% to 65% of your net monthly income

- Ensure that all your loans are repaid and cleared well before retirement

- Monitor the interest rate on loans. If you borrow ₹50 lakhs for 20 years at an interest rate of 9.5%, your total payment to the lender will exceed ₹110 lakhs, of which you will pay over ₹60 lakhs just as interest

REAL ESTATE INVESTMENT TRUST (REIT)

A Real Estate Investment Trust (REIT)—regulated by the Securities and Exchange Board of India (SEBI)—is an entity that owns and manages real estate properties with the sole purpose of pooling resources (like mutual funds) and generating income. Investors can purchase REIT shares in exchange for a percentage of the income provided by the underlying assets.

REITs distribute about 90% of their profits to investors. They generate income mainly by renting the properties. When property prices increase, the net worth of REITs automatically increases, which benefits the investors in the long run.

Real Estate Investment Trusts (REITs)

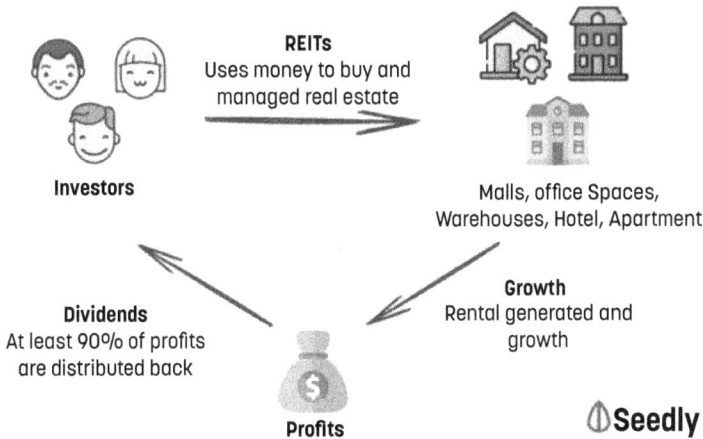

REITs
Uses money to buy and managed real estate

Investors

Malls, office Spaces, Warehouses, Hotel, Apartment

Dividends
At least 90% of profits are distributed back

Growth
Rental generated and growth

Profits

①Seedly

REITs ensure regular income as well as capital appreciation. They also enjoy tax benefits as they are exempt from paying income tax on the amount distributed to investors. Thus, REITs provide diversification and liquidity to investors. Since they are listed on exchanges, their shares can be freely sold or purchased in the open market. Because SEBI regulates them, transparency, professionalism, and good governance are assured. However, investing in REITs is always subject to market risk and fluctuations in the real estate sector. Despite these risks, the benefit of investing in REITs cannot be ignored, as they provide an opportunity to invest in properties without the need to acquire physical property. One needs to invest manageable amounts in REITs; you can start with a small amount as you are buying equities. It is advisable to conduct thorough research before investing in REITs.

What assets can a REIT own?

1. Real estate projects that earn rental income, including commercial projects such as offices, hotels, retail, industrial, and healthcare.

2. REITs cannot invest in residential houses, apartments, or speculative land banks.

3. At least 80% of a REIT's assets must be invested in completed and revenue-generating properties. The remaining 20% can be invested in under-construction properties or other permissible assets.

4. Leverage restrictions: Unit holder approvals are needed for debt-to-capitalization above 25%, and debt-to-capitalization is capped at a maximum of 49%.

Who can invest in Indian REITs?

1. Any investor (domestic, foreign, retail, or institutional) can buy REIT units in India.

2. There is no minimum trading lot size.

3. Investors can purchase REIT units using their Demat account on exchanges online or through intermediaries.

4. At present, there are a few listed REITs:

    • Embassy office parks

- Mindspace business parks
- Brookfield India REIT

SILVER

Traditionally, silver, often called as the "poor man's gold," has not been a favourite of investors as a pure investment. However, it is considered a safe asset to protect your wealth and act as a hedge in a volatile market. Historically, the price of silver has been more erratic than gold. See the following table:

YEAR	SILVER RATES IN ₹ PER KG.
2005	10,675
2006	17,405
2007	19,520
2008	23,625
2009	22,165
2010	27,255
2011	56,900
2012	56,290
2013	54,030
2014	43,070
2015	37,825
2016	36,990

YEAR	SILVER RATES IN ₹ PER KG.
2017	37,825
2018	41,400
2019	40,600
2020	63,435
2021	62,572
2022	55,100
2023	78,600
2024	75,500

The above table amply demonstrates the highly volatile nature of silver. It is more susceptible than gold because of its wide industrial applications. Silver is utilized in heavy industries, solar panel cells, cell phones, tablets, and many other products. Therefore, it fluctuates more than gold and heavily depends on economic conditions.

Many investors in India prefer silver as it is less expensive than gold, and it is also considered auspicious to buy silver on occasions of various festivals. Silver can be purchased mostly in physical form, though it can also be acquired through commodity exchanges as futures. This has been possible since 2021 when SEBI framed the rules for silver exchange-traded funds (ETFs).

You can buy silver in physical form, invest in stocks of silver companies, or invest in silver ETFs. Another way to invest in silver is to invest in mutual funds holding silver in their portfolio. Many experts opine that silver in one's portfolio does not bring any major advantage. Despite this, people do invest in silver. Even Warren Buffett, it is believed, has invested about one billion dollars in silver.

However, in general, you should invest in silver only if you expect a very high inflation rate or economic disaster. But the thumb rule is that your total investment in metals (including gold, silver, platinum, etc.) should be at most 10% of your total portfolio.

OTHER PRECIOUS METALS

Precious metals have charmed us since time immemorial. Do you want a ring that will be magnificent even after 30 years? Most probably, you do. Did you know that platinum is one of the few precious metals that will keep shining and stay white for 30–50 years, or even 100 years?

There is a reason why platinum rings are slightly more expensive than other white metal rings. You spend more for the durability of the platinum as compared to other metals—one that you will not have to maintain in the future, one that you can pass down through generations, and one that you will not have to worry about.

Gold and silver are the favourite of investors, but other metals are also catching their eyes recently. Platinum, whose availability is restrictive due to the complex extraction process, is trying to make its mark in the investment world.

What makes platinum a good investment avenue is the huge supply-demand mismatch. Globally, platinum output is a mere three million ounces, not even a tenth of the yellow metal's output. There are four ways you can invest in the platinum market globally. In India, we have only two options—platinum bullion, coins or jewelry, and futures trading on a commodity exchange. You can purchase bullion and coins from various centers such as banks and authorized dealers. The metal of 99.95% purity is usually available in 1 gram to 10 troy ounces.

Buying platinum by way of exchange-traded funds is not available in India. It is a versatile industrial metal with applications spanning from manufacturing to healthcare and jewellery. The World Platinum Investment Council (WPIC) states that the automotive industry, which uses platinum and other metals such as palladium in catalytic converters, has accounted for around one-third of worldwide demand during the last five years.

Palladium is a platinum group metal (PGM) and, thus, a "sister metal" to platinum. Unlike platinum and silver, palladium has a small jewellery market. The price of palladium, like platinum, is significantly more volatile than other precious metals.

OTHER INVESTMENTS

There are plenty of investment categories other than those mentioned above. Some of them are:

- Stones (like ruby, sapphire, and diamonds, etc.)
- Hedge funds
- Antiquities
- Art
- Collectibles like cars, boats, etc.
- Private equities (which are not listed on exchanges)

- Commodities
- Partnership and joint ventures
- Rare coins
- Fine wines
- Gambling
- Race course
- Options and futures
- Memorabilia
- Designer clothing
- Designer shoes
- Accessories like watches
- Holiday homes
- Insurance

Despite so many asset classes, the fundamental rule is to invest in what you know; as American investor Peter Lynch popularly said, "There is no point in buying something if you cannot liquidate the same when you need it." So consider all aspects like marketability, liquidity, returns, storage, ticket size, time horizon, etc. Know your limitations. Never go overboard.

BROAD ASSET CLASSES

There are four broad asset classes:

1. Equities and mutual funds
2. Debt instruments

3. Real Estate (including REITs)

4. Others (includes metal, commodities, private equities, art, collectibles, etc.)

Risk and reward in the above four types of asset classes may be understood as follows:

ASSET CLASS	RISK	REWARD
Equities and mutual funds	High	High to Medium
Debt instruments	Medium	Medium
Real Estate (including REITs)	Medium	Medium
Others	High	Low to Medium

ASSET ALLOCATION

Now, the million-dollar question begging for an answer is how much you should allocate to different asset classes. There is no readymade formula for this yet. It varies as per the needs and temperament of the investor. However, the following three points might help:

i. AGE

A young person may take more risks as the time is on their side. In the long run, say 15 years or more, equity has performed well and has given good returns compared to debt instruments. On the other hand, a person nearing retirement may be averse to taking risks and want to play safe. For that person, investment in equities will be less, and fixed-income instruments will be more. He might think of investing in metals, which are safe investments and act as a hedge against inflation.

ii. RISK APPETITE

It is the amount of risk a person is willing to take to pursue their goals. It would help if you struck a balance between risk and return. Some investors are aggressive by nature, while others are conservative. A conservative investor from a moderate background would like to invest more in safe investments.

So, if you are willing to take a certain risk, then plan to maximize your returns within that risk range. Conversely, what allocations must you adopt to reduce your returns?

iii. TIME PERSPECTIVE

If you want to invest in the short term, your portfolio should not be aggressive or dynamic. For example, if you intend to save to buy a car after three years, naturally, your preference will be liquid and safe investments. So much depends on your needs and goals.

SIMPLIFIED APPROACH TO ASSET ALLOCATION

Determining your asset allocation is not rocket science, though many complicated theories and sophisticated models exist. If a model is too complicated, people may not follow the same. Remember, simplicity is the key to brilliance. There is no hard and fast rule regarding how much should be invested in a particular asset class. It is subjective and depends upon the investor's age, time perspective, and risk-taking capacity. Compared to older people, youngsters can take more risks. Asset allocation creates a balance between risk and reward. First, you decide how much risk you are willing to take, and then you plan how to maximize your returns despite the risk.

Conversely, what allocation must you adopt to have an ideal portfolio? Experts widely advise the "100 minus age" rule. This means that the equity investment (direct stock and equity mutual funds) should be 100 minus the age of the investors. A 40-year-old can invest 60% in equity and the remaining in other asset classes. Conservatively, you may use the formula of "90 minus age". Of course, one cannot follow this or any formula blindly.

The following figures give a rough idea of your proposed allocation plan for those in their 30s, 45s, and 60s.

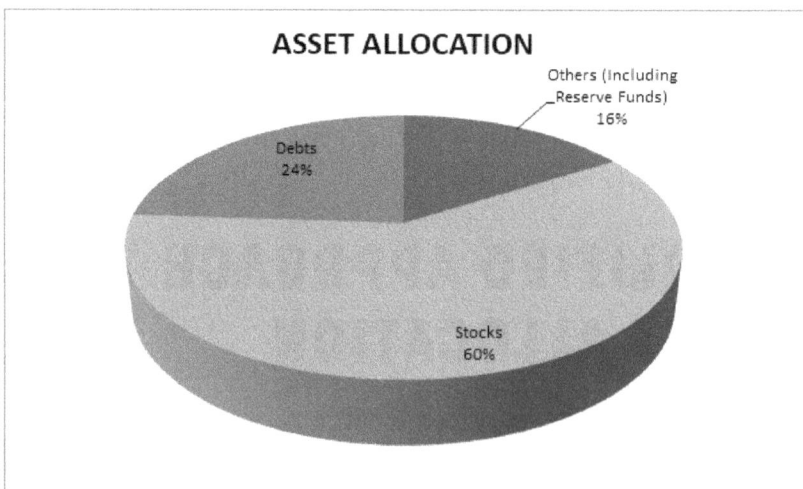

ASSET ALLOCATION

Others (Including Reserve Funds) 16%

Debts 24%

Stocks 60%

Asset allocation if you are about 30

ASSET ALLOCATION

Debts
33%

Others (Including
Reserve Funds)
22%

Stocks
45%

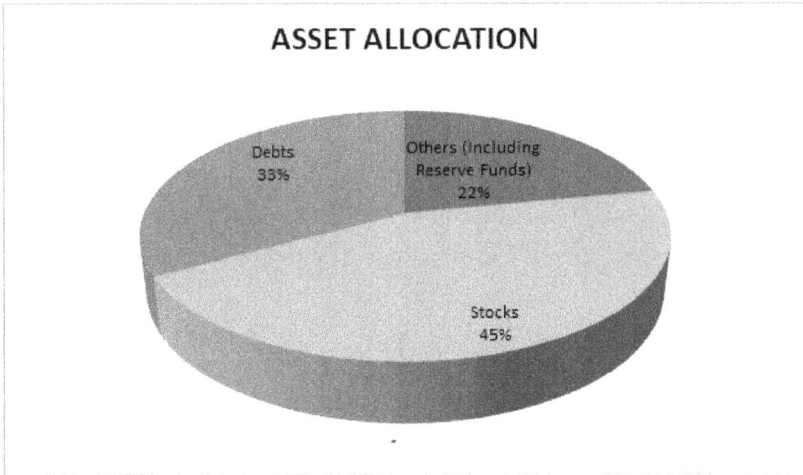

Asset allocation if you are about 45

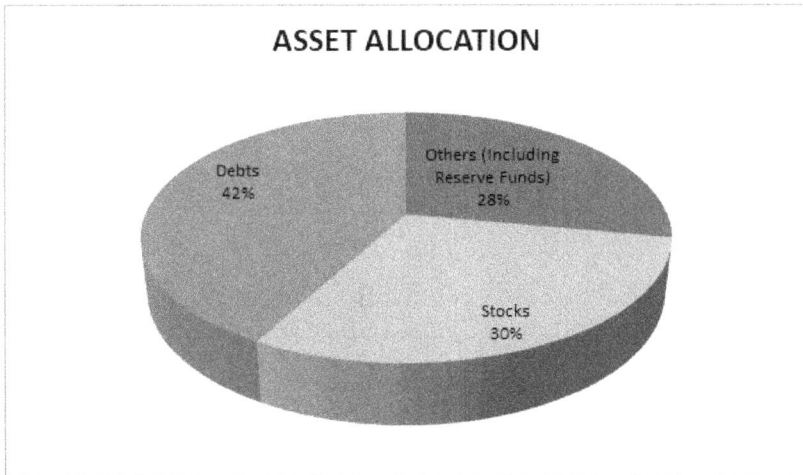

ASSET ALLOCATION

Debts
42%

Others (Including
Reserve Funds)
28%

Stocks
30%

Asset allocation if you are about 60

As mentioned earlier, you must consider your needs, goals, nature, and the time you can afford to remain invested. The examples below only will help you understand the importance of rebalancing and reviewing your portfolio. At the risk of repetition, your asset allocation plan should be tailored specifically to you. No two plans can be similar. In some cases, it may be wise to seek professional advice.

Let us understand the concept of asset allocation through a simple example—study Table A and B along with the notes provided below:

Table A
Your Investment as of March 31, 2023

ASSET CLASS	AMOUNT IN ₹
Equities and mutual funds (40%)	4,00,000
Debt instruments (30%)	3,00,000
Real estate (including REITs) (10%)	1,00,000
Others (20%)	2,00,000
Total	10,00,000

Table B
Value of your investment as of March 31, 2024

ASSET CLASS	AMOUNT IN ₹	PERCENTAGE IN YOUR PORTFOLIO	DESIRED VALUE IN ₹	EXCESS IN ₹	DEFICIT IN ₹
(1)	(2)	(3)	(4)	(5)	(6)
Equities and mutual funds (40%)	5,00,000	43.10%	4,64,000	36,000	—

ASSET CLASS	AMOUNT IN ₹	PERCENTAGE IN YOUR PORTFOLIO	DESIRED VALUE IN ₹	EXCESS IN ₹	DEFICIT IN ₹
Debt instruments (30%)	3,30,000	28.50%	3,48,000	—	18,000
Real estate (including REITs) (10%)	1,20,000	10.30%	1,16,000	4,000	—
Others (20%)	2,10,000	18.10%	2,32,000	—	22,000
Total	**11,60,000**	**100%**	**11,60,000**	**40,000**	**40,000**

Notes:

1. The allocation you have determined is 40% for equity, 30% for debts, 10% for real estate, and 20% for others (like metals). Table A above clearly indicates this.

2. Now, as of March 31, 2024, the value of equities has become ₹5,00,000, which makes your allocation towards equities 43.10% of the total portfolio of ₹11,60,000 (which is the valuation as of March 31, 2024).

3. As per your allocation plan, your valuation of equities as of March 31, 2024 should be 40% of ₹11,60,000, i.e., ₹4,64,000.

4. This means you now have excess investment of ₹36,000 in equities. So, to maintain the original allocation plan, you need to liquidate your equity investments worth ₹36,000.

5. Now, invest this realized amount of ₹36,000 in other asset classes, i.e., debts, real estate, and metals, to maintain the original ratio. This will ensure that your original allocation plan is consistently maintained.

6. Do not go overboard or act impulsively. If the difference is a minor amount, do not disturb that asset class. For example, in the above case, you may ignore the excess of ₹4,000 in real estate and instead invest it in debts or metals.

7. You need to review and rebalance your portfolio at least on a yearly basis; otherwise, your allocation plan will go haywire.

8. The figures mentioned in the above tables are for illustrative purposes only. They are not actual figures.

So, your adjusted investment portfolio now will look like this:

ASSET CLASS	% OF THE TOTAL PORTFOLIO	AMOUNT IN ₹
Equities and mutual funds	40%	4,64,000
Debt instruments	30%	3,48,000
Real estate (including REITs)	10%	1,16,000
Others	20%	2,32,000
Total	**100%**	**11,60,000**

The major benefit of asset allocation is that it allows you to purchase stocks when the market is low and sell when it is high. At the same time, you invest more in debt instruments and other assets when the market is high. This aligns with Warren Buffet's advice: "Be greedy when others are fearful; be fearful when others are greedy."

Thus, you maintain a mix of different asset classes. To create wealth and, at the same time, preserve it, ensure that you rebalance your portfolio annually. Many do so concurrently or on a monthly basis. As somebody rightly said, "Don't fall in love with your stocks; they can't love you back."

"Diversification may preserve wealth, but concentration builds wealth."

—Warren Buffet, American investor and businessman

CHAPTER 10

MULTIPLE SOURCES OF INCOME

"If your salary is your only source of income, you are one step away from poverty."
—Warren Buffet, American investor and businessman

WHY YOU MUST HAVE MULTIPLE SOURCES OF INCOME

Having multiple sources of income puts you in a commanding position in every walk of life. If you lose your job or if your business is not doing well, an alternative source of income can be a lifeline. If everything goes well, you accumulate surplus funds to invest, which ultimately helps you achieve financial freedom. You may clear your debts faster and retire early. After all, multiple sources of income create additional income and generate passive income in the long run. Other reasons for having multiple sources of income include:

a) You may want to quit your job and retire early.

b) To enjoy and maintain your desired lifestyle after retirement.

c) You work because you love to, not because you have to.

d) To serve society and help those who are less fortunate.

e) To travel around the world.

f) To develop hobbies and pursue passions.

g) To spend more time with your family.

h) To reach your financial goals faster.

i) To make money while you sleep.

j) To become debt-free.

k) To have financial security.

l) To ensure continuous income even after retirement.

Online courses, webinars, and online coaching classes mushroomed during the COVID-19 pandemic. Many people learned new skills, developed new hobbies, wrote books, and started online businesses.

Most of us have heard about the seven ways that rich people often make money: primary income, secondary income, capital gains, interests, dividends, rental income, and royalty income. Making extra money has become as simple as baking a pie in today's digital age. You don't have to put in long hours, nor do you have to invest a lot of money.

Who knows, your part-time hobby can become a lucrative full-time venture one day! Take the example of Chetan Bhagat, who used to write plays for his college events. After completing his MBA in marketing from Indian Institute of Management, Ahmedabad (IIMA), he worked with an international bank. He found the job monotonous, so he started writing again. His first book—*Five Point Someone*—was a runaway success. He discovered a new profession, and his first book has sold more than a million copies, which is unprecedented in Indian publishing.

Early in my career, I had a number of sources of income other than my main profession as a chartered accountant and financial advisor. I wrote several books on professional topics and contributed articles to professional journals, which provided me a decent honorarium. I also worked as a part-time examiner for professional institutes and worked as LIC agent. Of course, I no longer engage in these side hustles now, as I have achieved complete financial freedom.

So, identify the area of your passion, expertise, and what you enjoy doing the most, then, make a plan and develop a strategy. Build a strong team and network. Today, with the assistance of social media, you can launch a new business swiftly and with ease. You have all the tools you need to achieve your desires—your mind, body, emotions, intelligence, and above all, human existence.

If you are an extremely rich person and a few lakh rupees would not make any dent in your financial life, then this part is not meant for you. Please skip this section. But if you have just started your career or you have a moderate income, select a few multiple sources of income (not more than three) and find the best one suited to you.

If you are in your twenties, then saving about ₹5,000 per month could become ₹5 crores in 30 years if compounded at 12% per annum. You have to stretch yourself out of your comfort zone. Develop an empowering and self-serving habit. Follow a ritual. Many people say it is difficult to practice this. I do not disagree. However, with practice, grace, and firm commitment, it becomes possible. As American entrepreneur and author Jim Rohn has rightly said: "Every disciplined effort has multiple rewards." So has Dr. A. P. J. Abdul Kalam: "You can't change your future. But you can change your habits. Surely your habits can change your future."

FUNDAMENTAL RULES

The power of multiple sources of income is well understood and loved by those who aspire to be financially free. However, there are a few fundamental rules that you must follow:

1. Always remember that the universe does not give; it returns. It returns many times more than you give.

2. Go the extra mile. Always give more than you receive, as American writer Elbert Green Hubbard noted years ago, "Folks who never do any more than they get paid for, never get paid for any more than they do."[22]

3. Find your niche. What do you love to do? What is your unique selling point (USP)? You can't sell bakery products if you don't love cooking. You can't teach financial freedom unless you are financially free yourself.

4. Believe in what you do. You may have great talent, but if you don't believe in your talent, you will not take action, and therefore, you will not achieve success.

5. Be unique and add value to your services. Make it simple. As Indian spiritual guru Sadhguru says, "Making a simple thing difficult is not intelligence. Making a very complex thing simple is intelligence."

```
                      Talent
                    /        \
          Success              Belief
                    \        /
                      Action
```

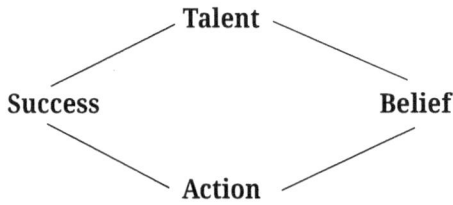

6. Canadian author and businessman T. Harv Eker says that rich people prefer to get paid based on results. They work on commission on percentage of revenue, choose stock options and profit-sharing in lieu of higher salaries.

7. Be a lifelong student. The more you learn, the more you earn.

8. Test your pilot project. If you are developing an online course, first invite your friends and give them a demo for free and take their feedback. Then implement their constructive suggestions in the course and launch it.

9. Start from whatever you have and wherever you are. My mentor Jay Kabir used to say, "Perfection kills the dream!". So, the dictum is *'kamate jao, sikhate jao'* (keep on earning, and keep on learning).

10. Maintain consistency and perseverance. Don't change your 'niche' area only because someone else is doing well in another area.

11. Don't be greedy. Focus on two or three workable ideas.

12. Put your activity on auto-mode by developing a system. For instance, investments in mutual funds are on auto-mode, but to develop a commission agency, you need to establish a system.

13. Protect your reputation at all costs. Build your brand. Increase your value. Be known on social media. Become an influencer. You might start your own blog or podcast which could generate extra income in the future. Blogs and podcasts are also useful for marketing your own products or services.

    You earn money by solving others' problems. With every prospective client you meet, think: "How can I solve the problem of so and so?"

14. Don't be afraid of competition. Learn from leaders.

15. Develop a team. You may start on your own, but you'll need to hire people when your business grows. Always remember that money is unlimited, but time is limited.

16. Lastly, don't forget to review your niche every year.

INDICATIVE LIST OF SOURCES OF MULTIPLE INCOME

You must find multiple sources of income based on your aptitude, expertise, training, and interest. However, a list is given below to help you realize that such sources are numerous. The list given below is indicative, not exhaustive.

1. Accounts writing

2. Acupressure or Acupuncture consultant

3. Affiliate marketing

4. Aerobics trainer

5. Airbnb (Rent your idle property)

6. Artwork selling

7. Animator

8. Anchor/ Master of ceremonies

9. Astrologer

10. App development

11. App tester

12. Ambulance service provider

13. Antique sales

14. Audio books

15. Babysitting

16. Become an angel investor

17. Become a franchisee

18. Become a singer

19. Beauty parlours

20. Biodata writing service

21. Cafeteria owner

22. Career counseling

23. Cartoonist

24. Car wash or rental

25. Charitable trust advisor

26. Clinical hypnotherapist

27. Create a job board

28. Create a newsletter

29. Coin and stamp collection

30. Content or Copywriting

31. Coding

32. Comedian

33. Commissioning agent

34. Computer consultant

35. Collaboration with other bloggers

36. Collecting e-waste or recyclables

37. Collecting blood samples

38. Consultancy in tax filings

39. Consulting geologist

40. Corporate trainer

41. Compose music

42. Crowdfunding

43. Credit Card advisor

44. Customized clothing business

45. Cybersecurity consultant

46. Dance coaching

47. Develop a subscription-based website

48. Driving instructor

49. Dropshipping business (become a vendor for third party)

50. Data analytics

51. Dietician

52. Digital signature distributor

53. Dispute resolution

54. Domain flipping

55. Dog walking

56. Electrician

57. Energy-saving consultant

58. Ethical hacker

59. Event management

60. Editing and proofreading services

61. Facebook advertising

62. Freemium business (basic course free and advance courses chargeable)

63. Feng Shui or Vastu consultant

64. Fitness coach

65. Financial consultant

66. Florist

67. Foreign exchange advisor

68. Garden maintenance

69. Games

70. Ghostwriting

71. Grocery supplier

72. Hair stylist

73. Hotel booking

74. Hotel concierge

75. Housekeeping

76. Healthy food suppliers

77. India-specific photography

78. Insurance agent or claim settlement

79. Investment in unlisted companies (Not to invest more than 10% of your total investment)

80. Investment advisor

81. Image consultant

82. Interior decoration

83. Lawn mowing

84. Leadership coach

85. Leave and license consultant

86. License a product idea

87. Liasoning with Govt. departments

88. Magnet therapist

89. Marriage consultant

90. Mass mailing services

91. Mementos and trophies suppliers

92. Mobile application developer

93. Modeling

94. Motivational speaker

95. Mutual fund distributor

96. Manage a BPO

97. Massage therapist

98. Marketing consultant

99. Marketing books

100. Mehendi designing

101. Network marketing or direct selling (choose the right company with a good track record)

102. Neuro-Linguistic Programming (NLP)

103. Newsletter publishing

104. Online courses or shop

105. Online data entry

106. Obesity management

107. Painting contract

108. Prepare LED banners

109. Preparing presentations for corporates

110. Paramedical professional

111. Part-time driving

112. Passport consultant

113. Pet trainer

114. Peer-to-peer lending

115. Pest control services

116. Photography for social media

117. Personal loan arrangement
118. Personal cook
119. Pranic healer
120. Press release services
121. Project finance consultant
122. Product designer
123. Podcasting
124. Polytechnic services
125. Poultry farming
126. Reading for blind
127. Real estate broker
128. Radio jockey
129. Reiki master
130. Registration of documents or will etc.
131. Resolution for labour disputes
132. Reviewing books
133. Remote surveillance
134. Royalty income from writing books
135. Sell digital courses online
136. Sell designed t-shirts
137. Sell high value items like jewellery, perfume, watches
138. Selling homemade products
139. Sell e-books
140. Sell nursery online

141. Sell your website or blog

142. Search engine optimization

143. Social media influencer (ensure good content, proper engagement, and consistency)

144. Sound management

145. Start an Instagram page

146. Stock market adviser

147. Stenographer

148. Stage decorator

149. Surveys

150. Writing subtitles

151. Teaching languages

152. Teach American accents

153. Telemarketer

154. Tiffin services

155. Tarot card reader

156. Tailor

157. Tattoo and piercing

158. Transcription services

159. Travel consultant

160. Translation services

161. Translating books

162. Tuitions

163. Used car seller

164. Vegetable supplier

165. Visa consultant

166. Videography

167. Voice-over artist

168. Volunteering in events

169. Video editing

170. Webinars and Workshops

171. Warehousing

172. Writing for visually impaired

173. Writing article in journals and newspapers

174. YouTuber

175. Yoga or spiritual or meditation teacher

Multiple streams of income are no longer a luxury; they are a necessity.

SETTING UP UMBRELLA FUNDS

"Build an umbrella fund while the weather is nice. Set up health fund while you're still healthy. Save for retirement while you're still young."

—Tony Robbins, American author and coach

Almost every financial advisor recommends generating passive income. They argue that financial independence is achievable only when you have passive income —when you don't work for money, but money works for you. However, I have noticed that many people have burned their fingers in the pursuit of passive income.

I'm not opposed to passive income. But before you even consider it, there are a few things you should do. Passive income without a strong security wall will eventually fail. My advice is to first take these steps, then plan your strategy for earning passive income.

Before doing anything else, ensure you have adequate term insurance and health insurance. These are covered in detail elsewhere in this book. Similarly, you must have an emergency fund, a reserve fund and a cushion fund and cash reserve while times are good.

A survey indicated that at least 75% of Indians do not have an emergency fund and could default on their EMIs in case of a sudden lay-off or any other event of income loss. The same was revealed in a survey by Finology Ventures, an affordable, subscription-based personal finance platform. Their report titled—*India's Money Habits 2023*—collected data from over three lakh Indians and revealed that one out for four Indians cannot even last a month if they lose their job. "Indians consider their parents and friends as their emergency fund! One in three has neither health insurance nor an emergency fund," said the survey.[23]

Another survey[24] tells us that 75% of Indians don't have adequate emergency fund. Additionally, 27% of Indians have neither a health insurance nor life insurance. Furthermore, 69% of Indians lack critical illness insurance, and 65% don't have accident death cover.

When it comes to debt, about 1 out of 6 Indians owes more than two times of what they own. As for retirement planning, we are significantly behind, with 68% of Indians not having planned for their retirement. The key takeaway is that one must take creating an emergency fund, reserve fund, cushion fund, and cash reserve seriously to have a turbulence-free journey towards financial freedom.

Once you have taken sufficient steps to protect yourself and your family through adequate insurance and health cover, you must proceed to maintain the following funds or reserves:-

Step 1: Establish an emergency fund to cover your essential expenses for at least three months.

Step 2: Establish a reserve fund equal to your six-month cash outflows.

Step 3: Create a cushion fund that cannot be less than three months in size.

Step 4: Maintain a cash reserve enough to cover one month's expenses.

Assume your monthly net income is ₹50,000, and your monthly essential expenses are ₹30,000. You would then need a ₹90,000 emergency fund, a ₹1,80,000 reserve fund, a ₹90,000 cushion fund and ₹30,000 in cash. These should be calculated keeping in mind essential expenses which are those without which you cannot survive. You can reach the above goal faster if you save consistently every month, including any extra money you may receive as a bonus, incentive, or through other income.

Your emergency, reserve, and cushion funds must be invested in liquid assets.[25] An emergency fund should only be used when there is an immediate, urgent need, such as job loss, business closure, health issues, or other unforeseen circumstances. Similarly, in severe situations (for e.g., to avoid heavy penalties, life-threatening circumstances, etc.), you may use the reserve fund.

Cushion funds provide you with relief when your emergency fund or reserve fund falls short. (The cash reserve should be kept in hard cash and does not need to be invested anywhere.)

It is critical that you clearly identify these funds. All returns and income from the above funds (except cash reserve) should also be invested in liquid assets. Remember that whenever you withdraw from these funds, you must replenish them as soon as possible.

I also suggest keep one or two credit cards in handy but use them only in case of emergencies. This provides extra comfort during an emergency. Many banks offer lifetime free credit cards. However, this is a double-edged sword. If you lack willpower and easily succumb to the temptation of buying things on credit card, then credit cards are not for you.

Once you've completed these previous steps, you're ready to embark on the journey of financial freedom. But make a note of the following:

1. Develop multiple sources of passive income. This is a slow process. Rome was not built in a day; it was built every day. As American rapper, entrepreneur, and activist Nipsey Hussle says, "Instead of trying to build a brick wall, lay a brick every day. Eventually, you'll look up and you'll have a brick wall."

2. Develop a corpus for specific goals and objectives. Once you have set your goal, work towards it. Make it your mission. A goal is nothing but your desire with a deadline. This has been discussed in detail in another chapter.

3. Achieve financial independence. The last step is to 'receive' and celebrate. Now that you are financially free, enjoy your life, do what you love to do, work on your passion and contribute for the welfare of your community.

> *"If you don't find a way to make money while you sleep, you will work until you die."*
>
> —Warren Buffet, American investor and businessman

CHAPTER 11

STOCKS AND MUTUAL FUNDS[26]

"The history of the stock markets tells us that they will surprise us in the future."

—Anonymous

We Indians love to save money. Historically, our savings ratio across different avenues has been quite good, ranging from 30% to 35% of the household disposable income for a long time. This clearly shows our aspiration to save. However, the next important step is to invest in the right avenues.

Many of us still tend to keep more money than necessary in banks, avoiding the stock market thinking that equities carry a higher risk. At present, only about 4% of the overall savings get invested in the stock market, with the rest in other instruments. There may be multiple reasons for avoiding stock market investment—it is an asset class that can deliver higher returns than other asset classes with the right time horizon and investment in the right place. Hence, you must recognize the stock market while building your investment portfolio. Let us understand more about it and decide whether it is for us.

STOCK MARKET AND ITS ADVANTAGES

Individual and institutional investors come together in the stock market to buy and sell ownership shares in publicly listed companies. When you buy shares of a listed company, you become a shareholder, which means you have a stake in that company and, theoretically, a claim on its profits and assets. Globally, stock markets play a vital role in enabling companies to raise capital and investors to build wealth over the long term.

Investing in the stock market offers several advantages for beginners and experienced investors. Let's discuss some of them:

1. **Wealth creation:** Investing in the stock market offers the potential for higher returns and wealth creation. If we look at S&P BSE Sensex since its inception on January 1, 1986, it has generated returns of 13.51% p.a. as of September 30, 2023. Even if we look at the last 10 years, i.e., from September 30, 2013, it is 13% p.a. Thus, the stocks have provided higher returns compared to many other investment options over the long term. Investing is a powerful tool to grow wealth and achieve financial goals, like retirement planning or funding major life events. No other asset class has the potential to deliver such high returns with such ease of liquidity.

2. **Diversification:** The large number of companies listed on the stock market provides many investment opportunities. You can invest across various sectors, industries, and companies; this allows you to spread your risk through diversification. Diversification of investments can mitigate the negative impact of poor performance by any single stock or sector.

3. **Liquidity:** Stocks are highly liquid investments, as buying or selling shares of publicly traded companies on stock exchanges during market hours is quite straightforward. The bigger the company, the more liquidity it has. This liquidity ensures that you can access your funds relatively quickly if needed.

4. **Long-term growth potential:** The Indian economy has been growing steadily over the years. In the last 30 years, India's average GDP growth rate has been close to 6.2%. In the coming years, India is expected to perform better as it progresses from a developing to a developed economy. The stock market tends to reflect this growth, and by investing in it, you can benefit from India's long-term economic expansion. We all have read about Foreign Institutional Investors (FIIs) and Foreign Portfolio Investors (FPIs) investing regularly in the Indian stock market because they recognize the potential to generate returns.

5. **Wealth distribution:** Stock market investors get the opportunity to participate in the ownership of companies, leading to a broader distribution of wealth across society. It allows people to invest in businesses, regardless of their background or socioeconomic status, and benefit from economic growth and prosperity.

6. **Regulation and oversight:** The Securities and Exchange Board of India (SEBI) regulates the Indian stock market. Over the years, SEBI has implemented regulations to safeguard the interests of investors and uphold market integrity. Thus, investing in the stock market is safer with the right information and advice.

The Bombay Stock Exchange (BSE) and National Stock Exchange (NSE) are two of the world's largest and most active stock markets in India.

BOMBAY STOCK EXCHANGE (BSE)

The Bombay Stock Exchange (BSE) is the oldest stock exchange in Asia, established in 1875. It is located in Mumbai and has thousands of listed companies. BSE's Sensex index consists of the top 30 companies listed on the BSE based on their market capitalization. Market capitalization is the total value of all outstanding shares of a company. For instance, if a company has 10 lakh shares trading at ₹2,000 per share, its market capitalization would be ₹200 crores.

NATIONAL STOCK EXCHANGE (NSE)

Founded in 1992, the NSE is India's largest stock exchange. Like the BSE, it is also located in Mumbai and has a significant number of listed companies. Nifty 50 is an index of the National Stock Exchange of India, comprising the 50 largest and most liquid Indian stocks based on market capitalization.

STOCK MARKET AND ECONOMY

The stock markets play an essential role in the growth of the Indian economy, particularly at this critical stage of progress and growth. The coming decade and a half can be among the most rewarding stages for Indian stock market investors. This is a widely discussed topic among fund managers and portfolio managers. The key is how much we, as retail investors, participate and make the most from this opportunity.

Let us examine the role the stock market plays in economic development:

1. **Capital formation:** Equities are a primary and significant source of capital for many companies. When companies come up with their Initial Public Offering (IPO), they plan to use the funds raised for various purposes like expanding operations, research and development, and infrastructure improvement. The goal is to invest the raised money to take the business to the next level and grow faster than at present. Capital raised in the form of equities contributes to economic growth and job creation across different sectors and industries.

2. **Business expansion:** When the money comes into the listed company in the form of capital, it provides the financial resources needed to expand its operations. This expansion in operations and efforts leads to more production, job opportunities, and economic development. This also helps in the development of many new regions and business hubs.

3. **Innovation and entrepreneurship:** India is one of the places where entrepreneurship is scaling up every day. We are constantly seeing more opportunities and innovations across different sectors and industries. At the same time, a new generation of well-established institutions is pursuing ambitious plans for innovations. The investors' money invested through stocks of the companies encourages entrepreneurship and innovation. As these young companies start progressing,

the stock investors of these companies also see the results in the form of returns.

4. **Job creation:** One of the biggest threats to the economy is unemployment. If people in a country are unemployed, it can trigger socioeconomic issues—this can be seen in many countries, particularly in the Middle East and Africa. The money raised by listed companies is often used to hire more employees to meet increased demand and support business operations. This makes a direct positive impact on overall job creation and income levels in the economy.

5. **Economic indicator:** The stock market has been viewed as a barometer of the economy's health. When the country's stock markets are performing well, it signals confidence in the economy and future growth prospects of the country and its people. You would have often heard people talking about the stock markets in the US, Japan, China, and Europe, as they also signify the progress of those countries.

6. **Increase in domestic consumption:** When the economy performs well, investors begin to see their wealth creation becoming more real. At the same time, with overall economic growth, the purchasing power of people improves, and so does their consumption. Those who earn more either from their businesses, jobs, or investments tend to spend more, and this results in further development of the economy. This creates a cycle where increased consumption leads to more production and job creation, giving more money to people.

Overall, stock markets are a critical component of a well-functioning economy. They provide a well-regulated and potential mechanism for raising capital, supporting economic growth, and distributing wealth.

However, it's important to understand that the stock market can be subject to volatility and risks. Therefore, we also need to be well aware of the associated risks and potential rewards before investing in equities.

INVESTING IN THE STOCK MARKET

Here is what you need to do before investing in the stock market, either on your own or with an advisor:

1. **Educate yourself:** Investing your money without knowing the avenue is like shooting in the dark. You should take the time to educate yourself about financial markets, investment strategies, and basic financial concepts. There are many books, online courses, and financial websites that can help you obtain more information and knowledge about the stock markets.

2. **Set objectives:** Investment is all about objectives. Whenever you invest in a particular company or multiple companies, it must have a purpose. Stock market investing is for the long term, regardless of what you hear or see around you. There are many data points to explain that the risk is higher in the short term, and the possibility of negative returns reduces as you hold good companies over the long term. Stock market investments are perfect for long-term goals like retirement planning, wealth creation, accumulating for children's education, and building a corpus to start your venture if this horizon is more than five years.

3. **Start slowly:** It is better to start slowly and then increase the investment as you gain more experience. Before starting, work on your budget that covers your mandatory regular expenses, and then work on an investment plan. This plan can include allocation in stocks directly or through equity mutual funds, but it has to be for the longer term.

4. **Open a Demat and Trading Account:** To invest in stocks, you will need a Demat and a Trading account. Many companies provide these services, and you can open your account through the one that suits your needs, offers competitive fees, and provides the resources you need to make informed decisions while investing. While dealing with broking companies, remember that investing in stocks aims to generate returns over time, and not to engage in activities like day trading.

5. **Understand the risks:** It's important to note that while there are multiple benefits to investing in the stock market, risks are also involved in equal measure. Stock prices can be volatile, and there are no guarantees of returns. Therefore, it's essential to conduct thorough research, diversify your portfolio, and, if necessary, seek advice from finance professionals to make informed investment decisions that match your financial goals and risk tolerance. Consulting with financial planners and investment advisors can help you build a comprehensive portfolio, and not just invest in the stock market.

6. **Consider mutual funds:** Investing in stocks on your own needs time, knowledge, and access to information. This may be challenging for most of us while we are busy professionally and personally. It is not just for the stock market but also for asset classes like debt, where one must have sufficient time

and knowledge to track the companies and interest rates. Here, mutual funds ensure you get the most out of your investments in any asset class without disturbing your professional work or family time. Mutual funds are among the simplest and easiest ways to invest, where you reap the benefits of returns from those investments.

MUTUAL FUNDS

A mutual fund is like a trust that pools the money of the investors for investing in different avenues. The professional fund manager then uses this capital to buy a diverse portfolio of bonds, stocks, or other securities. Each investor in the fund owns units that represent their proportionate ownership of the total holdings. Mutual funds depend on portfolio managers who are dedicated fund managers accompanied by a research team with the right experience and knowledge to manage the portfolio across different situations and market conditions.

ADVANTAGES OF MUTUAL FUNDS

1. **Professional management:** Mutual funds are managed by experienced professionals who make investment decisions based on extensive research and analysis. These portfolio managers and research analysts study companies and simultaneously visit many of these companies to gain a deeper insight. It is their full-time job to manage investors' money. Investors benefit from the expertise of fund managers who aim to achieve the fund's stated as per investment objectives.

2. **Diversification:** One of the most significant benefits of mutual funds is diversification. When you invest in a mutual fund, the fund manager invests your money in a broad range of securities based on their views and expectations. Ideally, one mutual fund scheme could invest in 25 to 100 companies, depending on the objective and the fund size. Whenever the portfolio is diversified, the risk associated with individual stock or bond investments reduces. This portfolio is diversified across companies, sectors, industries, market capitalization, and even geography. Managing a well-diversified portfolio with all these considerations may not be easy for individual investors. Hence, mutual funds offer the best opportunity to diversify, helping to spread risk and enhance portfolio stability.

3. **Ease of investing:** It is easy and convenient to start investing in mutual funds. Once you have worked on your budget, you must complete your KYC to begin investing. This KYC is common across all mutual funds and is the best part, unlike other avenues, such as banks, where every institution conducts its KYC. Different kinds of funds with defined fund objectives are available for investors. You do not need a large sum to start investing in mutual funds. You can start with a relatively small amount of money and build your portfolio over time. Imagine being able to invest in more than 25 to 50 selected companies every month by investing a few thousand rupees. Some mutual fund schemes allow you to invest as low as ₹500.

4. **Systematic Investment:** You would have heard about the Systematic Investment Plan (SIP). It is a simple way of building a huge corpus by investing a fixed amount regularly. SIPs allow you to benefit from rupee cost averaging. When the stock markets are up, you buy fewer units with your fixed

amount; when markets are down, you purchase more units. Over a longer period, this can reduce the average cost per unit, thus resulting in better returns. SIPs also make you a more disciplined investor, as your money gets invested automatically every month. Additionally, it also helps you harness the power of compounding as your invested money gets more time to grow further. SIPs are an excellent way for those who want to invest regularly in their financial goals. They work wonders for salaried individuals as well as business owners due to their systematic approach towards investing.

5. **Liquidity:** Most mutual funds are open-ended. You can buy or sell units of these funds on any business day at the fund's Net Asset Value (NAV). Usually, there is no lock-in period for mutual funds, except for investments in tax-saving mutual funds. This makes entry and exit from mutual funds much easier and hassle-free. If you need money in an emergency, you can easily sell the mutual fund units. Liquidity is an essential characteristic of any investment avenue, and in the case of mutual funds, they offer a significant ease of liquidation.

6. **Convenience:** Investments in mutual funds is a convenient way to grow wealth without investing in individual stocks. With mutual funds, professional fund managers handle investment decisions, asset allocation, and rebalancing, saving you time and effort. Moreover, you can seamlessly invest in mutual funds online and offline, making investing easy and hassle-free.

Advisors have a crucial role to play in building your portfolio based on your needs and objectives. A good advisor will help build the portfolio, monitor it regularly to ensure your investments are on right track, and suggests corrective actions wherever necessary.

TYPES OF MUTUAL FUNDS

Mutual funds offer different types of funds that can help you achieve all your financial goals based on your risk profile. Some of the most common and widely used mutual funds include:

1. **Equity funds:** These primarily invest in stocks or equities. They offer good growth potential and work well for investors with a long-term investment horizon. Equity-oriented mutual funds allow you to build a portfolio in the stock market without investing directly in individual stocks.

   There are different subcategories of equity funds, including large-cap, mid-cap, small-cap, flexi-cap, sector-specific, and international funds. As their name suggests, these funds invest in companies based on market capitalization or sector. Large-cap funds invest in well-established big companies, while mid-cap funds invest in companies in their growth stage, and some may become much bigger over a period. Small-cap funds mostly invest in companies that are at the nascent stage and have a much higher potential to grow. Flexi-cap funds invest across large, mid, and small-cap companies based on their prospects and is one of the most commonly invested categories within equity funds.

   Sector-specific funds invest only in particular sectors and industries, making these investments riskier as sectors or similar industries can go through business cycles depending upon country's fluctuating economic growth.

2. **Fixed-income or bond funds:** These funds invest in various debt securities like government bonds, corporate bonds, and municipal bonds. These funds typically carry less risk and are

less volatile than equity funds. They generate returns through interest payments based on the kind of securities the fund holds. When investing in fixed-income funds, there are two critical aspects to consider: first, the quality of the institution or company whose bond you are investing in, and second, the interest rate cycle, i.e., the outlook on how the interest rates will be in the future. Ideally, the fund manager takes care of this as they will closely monitor both aspects. The most common funds in fixed income are short-term, mid-duration, dynamic bonds, banking and PSU, corporate bonds, and long-duration funds. As their name suggests, the portfolio is constructed based on the fund's objective.

3. **Money market funds:** These funds invest in low-risk, short-term debt instruments like treasury bills and commercial papers. They are known for stability and liquidity, making them suitable for preserving capital and maintaining liquidity. These funds are predominantly for those who want to invest for shorter periods, such as a few weeks or months up to one year. These funds are mostly safe and do not carry much risk.

4. **Hybrid funds:** Also known as balanced funds, these funds invest in a mix of both equities and fixed-income securities. While hybrid funds carry less risk than equity funds, they offer better return potential than fixed-income or debt funds. These funds can work for those who seek steady growth in investment with limited risks. The most common hybrid funds are aggressive hybrid, balanced advantage, and multi-asset funds. In aggressive hybrid funds, the investment is predominantly in the stock market, which could be between 65 and 80%, and the rest can be in fixed income. However, among the hybrid funds, aggressive ones carry higher risk when

compared with other categories. Balanced advantage funds create a blend of equity and fixed income based on the view of the fund management team. Multi-asset funds invest across different asset classes, including gold and real estate.

Mutual funds provide an easy and accessible way to diversify your investment portfolio across different asset classes. These funds are managed by professionals who make investment decisions for you, reducing the burden of selecting individual stocks or bonds. While mutual funds offer many benefits, investors must understand the risks involved and conduct due diligence when selecting funds that match their financial goals and risk tolerance. The following section will discuss how to choose the right mutual funds for your investment strategy.

Selecting the right mutual funds is crucial for building a well-diversified and balanced investment portfolio aligned with your financial goals and risk appetite.

Here are some steps to choose the right mutual funds:

1. Identify investment objectives or financial goals along with timelines

Each financial goal holds significance and should be the starting point of your search for mutual funds. Mutual funds offer various options to help you invest in your financial objectives. You can start by defining and assigning the timeline to your goals. These goals can be short-term, like a vacation or buying a new vehicle, mid-term, like accumulating a down payment for a home, or long-term, like wealth creation, retirement, or children's education. Mutual fund investments work best when you avoid a mismatch in expectations.

For short-term goals, you can consider liquid, ultra-short-duration, and short-duration funds. Medium-duration debt funds, corporate bond funds, and banking and PSU debt funds can work well for your mid-term goals. Equity funds work best for your long-term goals.

2. Choose the right fund categories

The next important step is selecting the appropriate mutual fund based on your financial goals and risk appetite. Mutual funds offer investment opportunities across different asset classes, and within each asset class, there are different categories of funds. For instance, equity funds include index, large-cap, large and mid-cap, flexi-cap, mid-cap, and small-cap funds. Each category has a different approach to building and managing the portfolio. Here, the risk increases when you invest in portfolios with more allocation to mid-cap and small-cap. In debt funds, too, there are multiple kinds of funds, and their categories are based on the kind of institutions the money is invested in or the duration of the investment instrument. There can be a blend of categories in your portfolio, and that is fine, but the key is to choose the right kind of funds.

3. Fund house and fund manager

The role of the fund house and the fund manager is akin to that of an aircraft pilot, who must look into all aspects and generate returns for you. Understanding the fund house's philosophy and the fund manager's track record can help you select suitable funds for yourself. Many fund houses (for e.g., SBI Mutual Fund, HDFC Mutual Fund, Aditya Birla Sun Life Asset Management, etc.) usually offer funds in every category to ensure their presence and availability for investors, and there is nothing wrong with it. Each fund house has a style of managing money and offering its products. Some fund houses and managers may follow the aggressive approach, while others may prefer to focus on a few funds or adopt a conservative approach. Another aspect is fund manager's past performance and how long they have been with the fund house. You can also understand the process followed in managing funds with the help of the Scheme Information Document (SID), available on the website of the fund house.

4. Key details about the funds

The inception date or age of the fund, fund size (or assets under management—AUM), expense ratio, portfolio, and the riskometer of the fund are some indicators that provide crucial insights into a fund. The inception date can help you understand how old the fund is and how many stock market cycles the fund has gone through. Although the AUM should not influence your decision making, it does offer you information about the pool of investors investing in the fund. The expense ratio represents the total cost deducted from your fund value every day on a pro-rata basis, and this also affects the overall returns that you generate on your mutual fund investment.

All the funds have to publish their portfolio every month, which provides transparency on where your money is invested and offers insights into the quality of holdings and other details. The riskometer of the fund indicates the risk level associated with the fund, based on calculations related to the fund's portfolio and is more accurate to label. The riskometer can be used as a quick indicator of the fund's risk and whether it suits your risk appetite. All this vital information about the fund will help you decide on the suitable funds for yourself.

5. Performance across market cycles

While the fund's performance is one of the most preferred parameters for making an investment decision, you must look at long-term performance across different market cycles. Avoid taking a call by merely looking at the one-year performance or even just looking at the performance numbers. The real test of the fund is when markets are volatile or not in your favour.

Over the years, there have been many occasions where the stock market has gone through good and difficult phases. The track record of the funds across these cycles and their consistency will help you choose the suitable equity funds. Similarly, in debt funds, evaluating the fund's performance across different interest rate cycles will provide deeper insights into the debt funds.

You can use all these pointers to identify the mutual funds that will best help you work on your goals. Each point plays a significant role in the entire process of identifying suitable mutual funds for your portfolio.

There is no doubt about the important role stock market investing plays in today's world. It should be an essential practice across all age groups today, and avoiding it may not be the best decision. Therefore, anyone unable to invest on their own in the stock market should consider equity mutual funds to manage their investments. Many investors choose to invest both directly and through mutual funds; the key here is to have some allocation in stock markets.

"An investor without investment objectives is like a traveler without a destination."

—Ralph Seger, founder of the Provident Investment Management

CHAPTER 12

ENJOY GOLDEN YEARS OF YOUR LIFE

"The question isn't at what age I want to retire, it's at what income."
—George Foreman, American former professional boxer and entrepreneur

Whether you like it or not, your physical and mental capacity will decline with age. Few people are likely to have robust health even in their 70s and 80s. The vast majority of us will experience deterioration in functional memory, fitness, focus, and have problems in absorbing new information. Therefore, it is essential to take responsibility for planning your retirement and healthcare well in advance.

RETIREMENT PLANNING

To make life enjoyable after retirement without placing a burden on younger generations, start working towards it as early as possible. It is necessary to remain socially well-connected with friends and relatives. You must be emotionally, relationally, physically, and mentally sound to the extent possible.

Pursue your hobbies and passion for which you had no time before retirement. While you may slow down, you can still maintain a relaxed lifestyle. It need not be dreadful; rather, it's an opportunity to give back to society by way of helping less fortunate and spreading awareness about those subjects in which you have experience, knowledge, and mastery.

To start with, be extremely clear about the following:

a) Determine your current age.

b) Estimate your retirement age.

c) Number of years to reach retirement (b-a).

d) What you want to do after retirement?

e) Expected expenses per month at the time of retirement.

f) Adjust these expenses for inflation after retirement.

g) Calculate the corpus you will need to enjoy retirement without compromising your lifestyle.

h) Outline the steps you will take to remain physically, emotionally, relationally, and mentally fit after retirement.

i) Will you be staying alone or with family members?

j) What support system do you have in case of an emergency?

k) Would you like to drive your car even after the age of 70 or 80?

l) Are you associated with any social organization or an NGO?

The above information will ignite the passion to make your retirement years golden in true sense. Besides, you need to have following details in hand to create a retirement plan:

1. What is your current net worth? Refer to the chapter *Track Your Net Worth* and calculate your net worth meticulously.

2. Identify those items in the net worth statement that can and cannot be liquidated. For example, if you plan to transfer your residential property to your children, do not consider your house as an investment.

3. Develop your portfolio allocation plan, i.e., diversification of your investments.

4. Be conservative and calculate your retirement corpus.

These points will help in determining your corpus at the time of retirement so that you maintain a life free from financial worries. The relevant plan will vary from individual to individual. An extremely wealthy person may have a different retirement plan. A middle or upper-middle-class person cannot simply copy their plans. Each person's plan is unique; you are the best judge of your needs. There is no standard retirement plan which you can adopt instantly. Although all the chapters of this book will definitely guide you to chalk out a proper plan, but it is you who has to take decisions, actions, and accountability. Calculate your inflation-adjusted expenses and create a goal-oriented budget.

CALCULATE ESTIMATED EXPENSES AFTER RETIREMENT

Calculating your expected expenses per month after retirement is quite subjective and largely depends upon your lifestyle, family background, health status, and other factors. Expenses by their quite nature are unpredictable. In your golden years, you might have extra responsibilities, such as taking care of your family members or parents. Emergencies may come out of nowhere, but this should not deter you from planning. The general thumb rule is this that your expenses will double every 12 years. If you are currently 30 years old and plan to retire at 50 or 60, and your current monthly expenses amount to ₹25,000, then your estimated expenses at various stages of life might be as follows:

AGE (IN YEARS)	ESTIMATED EXPENSES (IN ₹)
30	25,000
42	50,000
54	1,00,000
66	2,00,000
78	4,00,000

The above calculations are based on the thumb rule and an assumed average inflation rate of about 6%. These figures will vary from individual to individual and largely depend upon economic situation at that time.

So, the question then arises: How much corpus will you need at the age of 50 or 60 when you retire? Once you know the figure, you can work backwards to build that corpus. You need not worry much about increasing expenses, as you will still benefit from compounding after retirement.

The return on your corpus may fluctuate over time, but what we are considering is the average return over a long period. Besides, to estimate the income as capital gain from other assets like real estate, metals, and collectibles is a herculean task. However, we will not dive into too many complexities, nor scratch our heads on what is Long Run Average Cost (LRAC), economies or diseconomies of scale, Minimum Efficient Scale (MES), or efficiency ratio and other technical terms. The more complicated a theory is, the less likely it is to be followed.

Simplicity is the ultimate sophistication. As a general rule, you must estimate your expenses on the higher side to ensure you have enough cushion to meet any emergencies.

If you have read the chapter on *Expenses Matter* carefully, it will be easier for you to understand your real monthly expenses. Revisit this chapter for a quick review.

If you plan to retire at 55 and expect to live up to 75, then you will have 20 years to spend in your retirement. These figures may change from person to person, but we work on the assumption that there are 20 years left after retirement. The corpus you require at the time of retirement may be determined by using an online calculator available on websites, such as Moneycontrol, Groww, Calculator.net, ClearTax, HDFC Life, and many others.

Remember, to calculate the corpus, you must input correct and realistic figures. If you put garbage in, you'll get garbage as a result. So, if you know your expenses, a thumb rule suggests that 25 to 30 times of your annual expenses is an acceptable retirement corpus.

HAVE A GOAL-BASED BUDGET

Most of us struggle to save because we think of it as a sacrifice of our immediate needs and wants. No wonder about 76% of Indians have no retirement plans. You will find many apps and calculators on internet help you understand and get an estimate on how much to save to meet a particular goal, but this has not motivated us to save. It's like constructing a building without any blueprint. Remember, everything happens in our mind before it appears in physical form. So, what is the way out? Simply have a blueprint of what you want. Create a goal-based budget which motivates and inspires you consistently.

If you have the right mindset and a burning desire that comes from within, you are in a better position to move towards financial freedom. That's why you will find the chapter on *Mindset* at the beginning. Take your own time and read that chapter thoroughly. Financial planning for retirement can't be done in haste.

Write down all your goals in the following manner:

A. My short-term goals are:

SR. NO.	GOAL	NO. OF YEARS TO ACHIEVE	AMOUNT REQUIRED
1.			
2.			
3.			
4.			

Short-term goals are those for which the time frame is of six months to three years.

B. My medium-term goals are:

SR. NO.	GOAL	NO. OF YEARS TO ACHIEVE	AMOUNT REQUIRED
1.			
2.			
3.			
4.			

Medium-term goals are those which you aim to achieve within three to seven years.

C. My long-term goals are:

SR. NO.	GOAL	NO. OF YEARS TO ACHIEVE	AMOUNT REQUIRED
1.			
2.			
3.			
4.			

Long-term goals are those which you desire to achieve any time after seven years.

Have personal goals that are unique to you, something you truly love. Never copy others' goals. Your life is different.

You may love to buy a luxury car while another person may like to enjoy a holiday abroad. Be clear on why you want to achieve this goal. One of my clients in Mumbai recently purchased a helicopter. Since he frequently visits his project site in Vadodara, this saves him time. Additionally, it creates a good impression on his partners, financers, and potential customers. Helicopter is not a luxury for him; it's a necessity.

Do this exercise: put this book aside and visualize your retired life. Feel it. See the minutest details. You are pursuing your hobbies. Perhaps you are writing your autobiography or simply a poem. You might be painting, gardening, playing with your grandchildren, spending time with a religious group, or volunteering with a local NGO. The list is endless. Once you start visualizing your retirement goals repeatedly, you will develop a deep desire to achieve them, which will put you into action. You'll begin preparing your retirement plan and start saving with a clear goal in mind. Make a budget at your earliest. You need not literally copy somebody else's budget, but I recommend following Li Ka-Shing budget model (discussed in the Chapter 5-*Expense Matter*). It gives you a fair idea of a balanced budget.

MAKE INVESTMENT YOUR PRIORITY

Once you have decided to save a certain percentage of your income, stick to it. Suppose you have determined to invest 20% of your net income, then diligently invest that 20% every month. I strongly advise you to increase your savings and investments by 10% each year. If you save ₹10,000 in the first year, save ₹11,000 in the second, ₹12,100 in the third year, and so on. The cumulative effect will be remarkable. However, this is subject to proportionate increase in your income. If your income is not increasing, then focus on earning more first, then save and invest.

Here's an example:

YEAR	NET INCOME PER ANNUM (IN ₹)	SAVING (IN ₹)	CORPUS (IN ₹)
1	50,000	10,000	10,000
2	55,000	11,000	21,000
3	60,000	12,000	33,000
4	65,000	13,000	46,000
5	70,000	14,000	60,000
6	75,000	15,000	75,000
7	80,000	16,000	91,000
8	85,000	17,000	1,08,000
9	90,000	18,000	1,26,000
10	95,000	19,000	1,45,000
20	1,45,000	29,000	3,90,000

Without the increment effect, the corpus will be only ₹2,00,000. Life is unpredictable; it may so happen that you are unable to save as per your plan. Sudden expenses may force you to deviate from your plan. My advice is, don't get disheartened or lose hope. Something better may also come along—perhaps an unexpected promotion or you may earn a huge windfall in the business, and sometimes we receive money from unforeseen sources. Always focus on the positive side of things. Think of abundance all around you. There may be several reasons for enjoying a retired life. Think about the following possibilities:

ENJOY GOLDEN YEARS OF YOUR LIFE

a) You might spend less during retirement.

b) Your children may do exceedingly well and support you.

c) Inflation rate may go down.

d) Your investments, whatever they are, may yield good returns.

e) You may earn more and save more in latter part of your life.

f) You may earn handsomely during retirement without devoting much time.

g) You may sell your house in the city and move to a smaller town.

h) You can mortgage your house and take out a loan.

The possibilities are endless. So, start saving with whatever you have, wherever you are, and whatever the situation is.

HOW MUCH TO SAVE?

The amount you need to save per month depends on your time horizon and income. See the following examples:

DESIRED CORPUS	INVESTMENT REQUIRED PER MONTH OF RETURN IF 10% P.A.			
	20 YEARS IN ₹	25 YEARS IN ₹	30 YEARS IN ₹	35 YEARS IN ₹
1 crore	13,060	7,474	4,387	2,612
3 crores	39,180	22,423	13,162	7,836
5 crores	65,300	37,372	21,936	13,061

THE IDEAL RETIREMENT PLAN

Nothing is permanent in life. Everything is changing and evolving. You can't predict what is going to happen 20 or 30 years down the line. But this must not stop you from planning your retirement. Of course, inflation will be there and purchasing power of money will decrease. And it is a fact that inflation hits more to the low-income and middle-income households. Then there is always uncertainty—be it economic slowdown, pandemic crises like COVID-19, wars, political instability, and so on. The list is endless. A prudent person factors inflation and uncertainty into their retirement plan to a reasonable extent.

One approach is that you may have a good corpus to spend during retirement, but many of us may like to preserve the capital and spend only the returns from our portfolio. You must choose which way to go as per one's own liking and attitude. In my opinion, an ideal retirement plan must guarantee sufficient passive income after retirement. However, in some cases, a part of the capital or corpus may be used.

We, Indians, are emotionally attached to our residential homes. Generally, we would not like to consider them as investments. In our country, an ancestral home is a source of pride for the new generation. However, here is a golden piece of advice: never transfer your residential house to your kids during your lifetime. Transfer it only through your will as a part of your estate planning. There may be exceptions, but it is valid for most of us. Imagine two situations:

a) House is in your name, and

b) House is in the name of your son

In situation 'a', your son might say, "I am staying with my father."

In situation 'b', he may say, "My father is staying with me."

Understand the difference.

In the annexures following this chapter, I have provided a few examples prepared in Excel sheets depicting how you can navigate your retired life with a certain corpus. If, at the time of retirement, your corpus is ₹1 crore and estimated expenses are ₹50,000 per month (which may increase by about 6% each year), you will have a comfortable retirement. But if your estimated expenses at the time of retirement are ₹2 lakhs, then you will need a minimum corpus of ₹3 crores. Please note, your active income, if any, has not been considered in this calculation.

If you want to preserve your corpus and spend only the returns arising out of it, the required corpus will substantially increase. You may use online calculators or Excels sheets to arrive at these figures. My advice is to make your retirement planning a personal affair. Excel spreadsheets are highly flexible and cost-effective tools. However, if you are tech-savvy, you may opt for any other tool as per your liking and experience.

A word of caution: Don't be obsessed with numbers like the amount of your retirement corpus. Life does not run on mathematics; it is a roller coaster ride. It works on emotions and aspirations. Things may not go as planned. Many experts advise, *"Plan your work and work your plan."* This wisdom looks good only on paper, you have to take the life as it comes. The truth remains that no saving is possible without income. So, your focus should be on your income and earning skills. Have multiple streams of income. Make your business profitable. Once you generate sufficient income, everything is possible—whether saving, spending, or investment. One of my clients, who is in the business of trading of chemicals, is still working at the age of 82—not because he has no savings, but because of his passion. He loves his business. He has modified his lifestyle accordingly; for example, he has shifted his office near his residence to save commuting time. He works four hours a day and takes weekends off. The system works for him now. He has an active as well as passive income. The point is that you cannot solely rely on your *passive* income. Have *passion* income as well.

At the age of 25 or 30, determining the year of retirement is like firing in the dark. Who knows when you will retire? An Excel sheet can't decide your date of retirement. While the company or organization you are working with may have retirement age, but it is not the end of your life. I know numerous individuals whom companies have rehired as consultants or advisors after their retirement. If you are skilled and physically fit, there will be plenty of opportunities and openings for you.

I am not suggesting that you slog till your last breath. What I am highlighting is that let your potential be fruitfully utilized even after the so-called retirement. As American author and motivational speaker Wayne Dyer aptly says, "Either you do what you love or love what you do."

"Your best retirement plan for retiring happy and prosperous—
don't be a burden on others."
—Ernie J Zelinski, author of *How to Retire*
Happy, Wild, and Free

Retirement Planning Model-1

YEAR AFTER RETIREMENT	OPENING CORPUS	INCOME (12% P.A.)	TAX (15% ON INCOME)	NET INCOME AFTER TAX	WITHDRAWALS	WITHDRAWALS FOR SPECIFIC PURPOSE AND URGENCIES	CHARITY (OPTIONAL)	IN LAKH NET CLOSING
			1	2	3	4	5	(2-3-4-5)
1	100	12	2	10	6	0	1	103
2	103	12	2	10	6	0	1	106
3	106	13	2	11	7	5	1	104
4	104	12	2	10	7	0	1	106
5	106	13	2	11	7	0	1	109
6	109	13	2	11	8	5	1	106
7	106	13	2	11	8	0	1	108
8	108	13	2	11	8	0	1	110

1-CRORE CORPUS PLAN

1-CRORE CORPUS PLAN

								IN LAKH
YEAR AFTER RETIREMENT	OPENING CORPUS	INCOME (12% P.A.)	TAX (15% ON INCOME)	NET INCOME AFTER TAX	WITHDRAWALS	WITHDRAWALS FOR SPECIFIC PURPOSE AND URGENCIES	CHARITY (OPTIONAL)	NET CLOSING
			1	2	3	4	5	(2-3-4-5)
9	110	13	2	11	9	5	1	106
10	106	13	2	11	9	0	1	107
11	107	13	2	11	9	0	1	108
12	108	13	2	11	10	5	1	103
13	103	12	2	10	10	0	1	102
14	102	12	2	10	10	0	1	101
15	101	12	2	10	11	5	1	94
16	94	11	2	9	11	0	1	91
17	91	11	2	9	11	0	1	88

1-CRORE CORPUS PLAN

IN LAKH

YEAR AFTER RETIREMENT	OPENING CORPUS	INCOME (12% P.A.)	TAX (15% ON INCOME)	NET INCOME AFTER TAX	WITHDRAWALS	WITHDRAWALS FOR SPECIFIC PURPOSE AND URGENCIES	CHARITY (OPTIONAL)	NET CLOSING
			1	2	3	4	5	(2-3-4-5)
18	88	11	2	9	12	5	1	79
19	79	9	1	8	12	0	1	74
20	74	9	1	8	12	0	1	69
21	69	8	1	7	13	5	1	57
22	57	7	1	6	13	0	1	49
23	49	6	1	5	13	0	1	40
24	40	5	1	4	14	5	1	24

Retirement Planning Model-2

3-CRORE CORPUS PLAN

IN LAKH

YEAR AFTER RETIREMENT	OPENING CORPUS	INCOME (12% P.A.)	TAX (15% ON INCOME)	NET INCOME AFTER TAX	WITHDRAWALS	WITHDRAWALS FOR SPECIFIC PURPOSE AND URGENCIES	CHARITY (OPTIONAL)	NET CLOSING (2-3-4-5)
			1	2	3	4	5	
1	300	36	5	31	25	0	1	305
2	305	37	6	31	26	0	1	309
3	309	37	6	31	26	8	1	305
4	305	37	6	31	27	0	1	308
5	308	37	6	31	27	0	1	311
6	311	37	6	31	28	8	1	305
7	305	37	6	31	28	0	1	307
8	307	37	6	31	29	0	1	308

3-CRORE CORPUS PLAN

IN LAKH

YEAR AFTER RETIREMENT	OPENING CORPUS	INCOME (12% P.A.)	TAX (15% ON INCOME)	NET INCOME AFTER TAX	WITHDRAWALS	WITHDRAWALS FOR SPECIFIC PURPOSE AND URGENCIES	CHARITY (OPTIONAL)	NET CLOSING
			1	2	3	4	5	(2-3-4-5)
9	308	37	6	31	29	8	1	301
10	301	36	5	31	30	0	1	301
11	301	36	5	31	30	0	1	301
12	301	36	5	31	31	8	1	292
13	292	35	5	30	31	0	1	290
14	290	35	5	30	32	0	1	287
15	287	34	5	29	32	8	1	275
16	275	33	5	28	33	0	1	269
17	269	32	5	27	34	0	1	261

3-CRORE CORPUS PLAN

IN LAKH

YEAR AFTER RETIREMENT	OPENING CORPUS	INCOME (12% P.A.)	TAX (15% ON INCOME)	NET INCOME AFTER TAX	WITHDRAWALS	WITHDRAWALS FOR SPECIFIC PURPOSE AND URGENCIES	CHARITY (OPTIONAL)	NET CLOSING
			1	2	3	4	5	(2-3-4-5)
18	261	31	5	26	34	8	1	244
19	244	29	4	25	35	0	1	233
20	233	28	4	24	35	0	1	221
21	221	27	4	23	36	8	1	199
22	199	24	4	20	36	0	1	182
23	182	22	3	19	37	0	1	163
24	163	20	3	17	37	8	1	134

Retirement Planning Model-3

5-CRORE CORPUS PLAN

IN LAKH

YEAR AFTER RETIREMENT	OPENING CORPUS	INCOME (12% P.A.)	TAX (15% ON INCOME)	NET INCOME AFTER TAX	WITHDRAWALS	WITHDRAWALS FOR SPECIFIC PURPOSE AND URGENCIES	CHARITY (OPTIONAL)	NET CLOSING
			1	2	3	4	5	(2-3-4-5)
1	500	60	9	51	31	0	1	519
2	519	62	9	53	32	0	1	539
3	539	65	10	55	34	25	1	535
4	535	64	10	54	36	0	1	552
5	552	66	10	56	38	0	1	569
6	569	68	10	58	40	25	1	561
7	561	67	10	57	42	0	1	575
8	575	69	10	59	44	0	1	590

5-CRORE CORPUS PLAN								IN LAKH
YEAR AFTER RETIREMENT	OPENING CORPUS	INCOME (12% P.A.)	TAX (15% ON INCOME)	NET INCOME AFTER TAX	WITHDRAWALS	WITHDRAWALS FOR SPECIFIC PURPOSE AND URGENCIES	CHARITY (OPTIONAL)	NET CLOSING
			1	2	3	4	5	(2-3-4-5)
9	590	71	11	60	46	25	1	578
10	578	69	10	59	48	0	1	587
11	587	70	11	59	51	0	2	594
12	594	71	11	60	53	25	2	574
13	574	69	10	59	56	0	2	575
14	575	69	10	59	58	0	2	574
15	574	69	10	59	60	25	2	546
16	546	65	10	55	62	0	2	537
17	537	64	10	54	64	0	2	525

5-CRORE CORPUS PLAN

IN LAKH

YEAR AFTER RETIREMENT	OPENING CORPUS	INCOME (12% P.A.)	TAX (15% ON INCOME)	NET INCOME AFTER TAX	WITHDRAWALS	WITHDRAWALS FOR SPECIFIC PURPOSE AND URGENCIES	CHARITY (OPTIONAL)	NET CLOSING
			1	2	3	4	5	(2-3-4-5)
18	525	63	9	54	66	25	2	486
19	486	58	9	49	68	0	2	465
20	465	56	8	48	70	0	2	441
21	441	53	8	45	72	25	2	387
22	387	46	7	39	74	0	2	350
23	350	42	6	36	76	0	2	308
24	308	37	6	31	78	25	2	234

Please note:
1. The figures used in these tables are only indicative. They may change based upon individual requirements, temperament, market conditions, and risk appetite.
2. All figures are in lakhs.
3. Return has been assumed at 12% per annum and average tax is taken at 15%.
4. Withdrawal includes premium for insurance including mediclaims.
5. Withdrawals have been taken at 60% of net income and thereafter yearly increase of 6%.

CHAPTER 13

TAX PLANNING[27]

"The hardest thing in the world to understand is the income tax."
—Albert Einstein, Theoretical physicist

Two things are certain in life: death and taxes. However, while life ends with death, the same cannot be said about taxes. As long as income is generated by the assets of the deceased person, income tax will continue to apply.

Income tax is a broad and complicated subject, even for professionals, let alone laypeople. However, it is essential for a layperson to understand the basics of what avenues are available under the law to save taxes. Tax planning requires to be aligned with your overall financial goals. It can only act as an incentive to do the right thing. What matters is how sound your financial planning is—investing in a poor fund or other assets just to get some tax benefits makes no sense. It will be penny-wise and pound-foolish.

So, it is best to avoid considering tax planning as a be-all and end-all. That said, remember that the taxman will always take more if you let him. Taxes can wipe out your gains by 20 to 30%. It is worth trying if you can save half of that through proper planning.

The most critical sections under The Income Tax Act, 1961 for individuals are Sections 80C, 80D, and 80E.

SECTION 80C

This section is the most common and well-known among taxpayers. Under this section, a maximum of ₹1,50,000 is deductible from the gross total income of a taxpayer. Common investment options under this section are:

a) Employees' Provident Fund (EPF) and Voluntary Provident Fund (VPF)

b) Public Provident Fund (PPF)

c) National Savings Certificate (NSC)

d) Bank deposits

e) Life Insurance premium

f) Equity Linked Saving Scheme (ELSS)

g) Senior Citizen Savings Schemes (SCSS)

h) Housing loan principal

i) School tuition fees for children

Since many of you are already aware of the provisions of this section, I will not delve into its details. However, I want to highlight some aspects that the majority may not be aware of.

NATIONAL SAVING CERTIFICATE (NSC)

Interest on the same is taxable on an accrual basis, meaning it must be reported as income each year. However, the accrued interest can also be claimed under Section 80C, except for last year's interest. It is observed that while taking deductions, people often invest in NSC, but in subsequent years, they forget to include the accrued interest in their taxable income. This oversight becomes apparent only when the maturity receipts are reflected in the bank statement.

TAX-SAVING BANK FIXED DEPOSITS

There is a lock-in period of five years, and you cannot avail of any loan facility against these fixed deposits. Interest earned on these fixed deposits is also taxable.

LIFE INSURANCE PREMIUM

Not all life insurance premiums paid are eligible for deduction under Section 80C. Verify the eligibility before taking out insurance. If you surrender the policy within two years, then the benefit claimed in earlier years is reversed. GST paid on the premium is not eligible for deduction. Typically, LIC issues a covering letter at the time of insurance maturity, which should be preserved if you have claimed the maturity proceeds as exempt under Section 10(10D) of the Income Tax Act. In the case of other insurers, they may send emails intimating the maturity of the insurance. This also should be preserved carefully to substantiate the exemption under Section 10(10D). Further, deductions are available on an actual payment basis. For instance, if the FY 2022-23 insurance premium is paid during FY 2023-24, then the deduction for the same would be eligible for FY 2023-24.

HOUSING LOAN

The principal payment of the loan is covered under this section. However, if you sell the house within five years, then the benefit claimed earlier is reversed. If the house is under joint names, then the loan should also be in joint names so that all joint holders can claim income tax deductions. Furthermore, all joint holders should contribute to the EMI payments. If the EMI is only paid by one holder, then the deduction claimed by the other holders may be denied. It's advisable to open a joint account consisting of all the holders, where all the joint holders can contribute their share, and the EMI is debited from this account.

SCHOOL FEES

This deduction is restricted to two children. Additionally, only tuition fees are allowed. Other fees, such as computer fees, uniform fees, bus charges, donations, etc., are not allowed. So, it is advisable to review the school fees receipt where the school provides a breakup of the fees, rather than summing up the figure from the bank statements.

SECTION 80D

In case of taxpayers below 60 years of age:

- If all family members are below 60 years of age, a maximum deduction of ₹25,000 can be claimed. An additional ₹25,000 can be claimed in respect of parents, who are *below 60 years* of

age. Thus, the maximum deduction one can claim in this case is
₹50,000

- Apart from a maximum deduction of ₹25,000, an additional of
  ₹50,000 can be claimed if taxpayers' parents are *above 60 years*
  of age. Thus, the maximum the tax payer can claim is ₹75,000
  in this case

- However, if one of the family members is above 60 years,
  then a maximum of ₹50,000 can be claimed for self and family
  members. An additional ₹50,000 can be claimed in respect of
  parents, who are above 60 years of age, making the maximum
  deduction ₹1,00,000

In case of taxpayers above 60 years of age:

- A maximum deduction of ₹50,000 can be claimed for self
  and family member. An additional ₹50,000 can be claimed in
  respect of parents, who are also above 60 years of age, making
  the maximum deduction ₹1,00,000

Additionally, a taxpayer who incurs medical expenditure for self,
family members, or parents is eligible for a deduction of up to ₹50,000
under this section. Here, the condition is that the person on whom the
expenditure is incurred should be a senior citizen, and the taxpayer
should not have incurred any expenditure towards a Mediclaim
policy for that person. Here, 'family' means spouse and dependent
children of the taxpayer.

Here, too, GST paid on the insurance premium is not eligible for
deduction. Payments made in cash are not eligible, except preventive
health check-up payments, which can be made by any mode,
including cash. However, the deduction is limited only to ₹5,000. In
the case of a single health insurance premium covering more than

one year, the deduction shall be proportionately allowed based on the number of years for which health insurance coverage is provided.

SECTION 80E

Deduction for interest on loans taken for higher education is also deductible. However, there is a controversy as to whether education loan taken for studying abroad is covered or not. Here, there is no limit with respect to the amount of deduction for interest paid towards the loan. It is available from the year the taxpayer starts paying the interest and seven immediate succeeding years.

SECTION 80EEB

Deduction in respect of interest paid on loans taken for purchasing an electric car is eligible for up to ₹1,50,000. However, please note that this deduction is not available in respect of the purchase of a hybrid car on loan.

SECTION 80G

Any individual who donates money is eligible for a deduction of 50 to 100% of the amount paid. The deduction is limited to 10% of the adjusted gross total income for certain donations. Any donation in cash exceeding ₹2,000 is not be allowable as a deduction. Additionally, the ARN (document reference number) needs to be mentioned in the return of income if the donation is made to entities where 50%

deductions are eligible. Otherwise, the return of income cannot be validated.

SECTION 80GG

In the case of non-salaried taxpayers who stay in rental accommodation, a deduction of up to taxpayer 5,000 per month can be claimed under this section.

SECTION 80CCD(IB)

Deductions of up to ₹50,000 are available for investment in the NPS. This is an additional deduction over and above the normal ceiling limit of ₹1,50,000 under Section 80CCCD (IB).

SECTION 24(B)

Interest paid or payable on the amount borrowed for purchasing a house property is allowed as a deduction while computing income under the head 'House Property.'

Where the individual lets out a house property, the amount of interest paid or payable on the loan taken to purchase such house is allowed as a deduction without any limit.

The full deduction is allowed for the interest paid or payable on the loan taken to purchase a house that is deemed to be let out during the relevant financial year.

In respect of self-occupied house property, the individual can claim an aggregate amount of deduction of up to ₹2,00,000 towards the interest paid or payable on the loan taken to purchase or construct such property.

The interest is allowed as a deduction on an accrual basis and it can be claimed as a deduction even if it is not actually paid during the year.

If a fresh loan is taken to repay the earlier loan taken for the aforesaid purpose, the interest payable in respect of the second loan is also admissible as a deduction.

ADVANCE TAX

The law requires that at the beginning of the financial year (April to March), a taxpayer must estimate their income for the year. Based on this, they must calculate the tax payable. Here, 'tax payable' refers to tax on income minus TDS. This is the balance tax payable by the taxpayer. They must discharge this balance through advance tax payments during the financial year as follows:

On or before June 15	15% of total tax
On or before September 15	45% of total tax
On or before December 15	75% of total tax
On or before March 15	100% of total tax

There are a few exceptions where the above provisions are not applicable or are applied more liberally. For example, in the case of a person above the age of 60 not earning business income, advance tax provisions do not apply. Thus, it would be prudent to estimate the income an individual is likely to earn during the year and then consult his CA regarding the applicability of advance tax provisions. The reason is, in case of default, interest at of 1% per month is applicable on the shortfall in payment of advance tax, translating to 12% per annum. It should be noted that in the case of refunds, the government pays a yearly interest at 6%. Therefore, interest on default in payment of advance tax at 12% per annum will increase our tax outflow, which could have been easily avoided.

SELF-ASSESSMENT TAX

If there is any balance tax payable, it can be discharged when filing a tax return. However, tax returns must be filed within the due date. In case of a delay in filing tax returns, further interest may be levied on the balance tax payable. Additionally, late fees of up to ₹5,000 may be charged if filed before December. If even a belated return is not filed and there is tax payable, updated returns can be filed by paying up to 50% more in taxes. The department may also launch prosecution proceedings for not filing the return. Thus, it would be prudent to file tax returns on time to avoid unwarranted consequences.

NEW TAX REGIME

The Finance Act of 2020 has introduced a new tax regime for individuals and Hindu Undivided Families (HUFs), known as the alternate tax regime, which is governed by Section 115BAC. This regime allows individuals and HUFs the option to pay tax at lower rates; however, they must forego certain exemptions and deductions which are otherwise available to them under the old tax regime. The new tax regime is optional. Therefore, an individual or HUF must evaluate the tax payable under both schemes every year and choose the more beneficial one. It should be noted that for individuals and HUFs with business income, if they opt to be governed by the new scheme, they can opt out only once.

The decision to opt for the alternate tax regime depends on the amount of exemptions and deductions available to the individual or HUF. If an individual has no deductions available to them under the old tax regime, it would generally be more beneficial to them to opt for the new tax regime. However, many individuals are paying insurance premiums, children's education expenses, PPF, medical claims, housing loans, etc. Thus, it is imperative to calculate the tax under both schemes and choose the one that is more beneficial.

Further, the basic exemption limit under the new tax regime for all resident individuals is ₹3,00,000 but taxes are lower. Under Old Tax regime, basic exemption for a *resident* individual up to 60 years is ₹2,50,000. For individuals between the age of 60 and 80, the basic exemption is ₹3,00,000; for those above 80 years, it's ₹5,00,000 but taxes are higher.

Under the old tax regime, a rebate under Section 87A is available to a *resident* individual whose total income during the previous year is below ₹5,00,000. This means that, if during the previous year, an individual's income is up to ₹5,00,000, they need not pay any tax. However, if their income is more than ₹2,50,000 but below ₹5,00,000, they are compulsorily required to file a tax return.

Under the new tax regime, a rebate under section 87A is available to a *resident* individual whose total income during the previous year is below ₹7,00,000. This means that if an individual's income is up to ₹7,00,000, they need not pay any tax. However, if their income is more than ₹2,50,000 but below ₹7,00,000, they are required to file a tax return.

Section 115BAC has been amended by the Finance Act 2023 to provide more incentives in the new tax scheme so that the taxpayers unhesitatingly transition from the old to the new tax scheme. The Finance Act 2023 has also inserted a new sub-section (6) to Section 115BAC, making the new tax scheme the default scheme for eligible assessees. If the eligible assessee wants to pay tax as per the old regime, they must opt out of the new tax scheme in a prescribed manner. In the case of salaried employees, they need to inform their employers about their choice. If they don't, then as per guidelines, the employer will deduct TDS as per the new scheme, as this has been made the default scheme.

Section 115BAC has been further amended by the Finance Act 2024 to enhance the amount of following deductions:

Standard deduction from salary has been increased from ₹50,000 to ₹75,000.

Deduction for family pension has been increased from ₹15,000 to ₹25000.

HOW TO OPT FOR AN OLD TAX REGIME

An individual not earning business income can switch between the old and new schemes every year.

Deductions under Chapter VI-A (except deduction available under section 80CCD (2), i.e., employer's contribution towards NPS, deduction under Sections 80JJAA and 80LA(1A)) are not available.

Deductions or exemptions under Sections 10(5) / (13A) / (14) / (17) / (32), 16, 24(b) and 57(iiia) are not available (except deduction under Section 24(b) pertaining to let-out property or deemed let-out property is available). Furthermore, brought-forward losses pertaining to these deductions or exemptions cannot be set off and carried forward. Even loss in current house property cannot be set off against any other income.

The individual must opt for the old scheme by filing Form 10IEA on or before the due date of filing their return.

In case of an assessee earning business income, the option, once exercised for any previous year, can be withdrawn only once. Thereafter, the person shall never be eligible to exercise the option under Section 115BAC (except where such person ceases to have any business income).

DIVERSION OF INCOME

Suppose an individual has a salary income of ₹7,00,000 and an investment of ₹20,00,000 in bank fixed deposits earning interest, for example, at an annual rate of 8%. In this case, interest income amounts to ₹1,60,000 per annum. Thus, his total income comes to ₹8,60,000. The tax the individual has to pay would be ₹42,640.

In this case, tax planning could involve gifting the sum of ₹20,00,000 to their parents or adult child. Fixed deposits should be taken in the parent's name (eligible for higher interest rate in the case of a senior citizen) or adult child's name. Thus, both would end up not paying any taxes, thereby saving a tax of ₹42,640. Remember to nominate yourself in the fixed deposit investments. Do not gift to your spouse, as this would attract clubbing provisions, and the interest income would be clubbed in the hands of the transferor. If you don't have the above options, the alternative would be to give the sum at a low-interest rate to your wife or HUF. In this case, your wife or HUF would receive interest at 8%, whereas you will receive a lower rate of interest, which would be added to your income. In this manner, you would make a saving of tax on the difference earned by you and your wife or HUF.

DISCLOSURE

It is mandatory to disclose all incomes, whether taxable or non-taxable, in the income tax return. So, let's say you receive a sum from maturity of a Public Provident Fund Account (PPF); then the same should be disclosed as exempt income in the return of income. The same applies to the amount received as a gift from relatives, maturity of insurance policies, etc.

AGRICULTURAL INCOME

Many have the misconception that income from agriculture is exempt. Agricultural income in India is generally exempt from tax under Section 10(1) of the Income Tax Act, 1961. However, when a person has both agricultural and non-agricultural income, the agricultural income may indirectly affect the tax liability through a concept called "partial integration." Here agricultural income and non-agricultural income are combined for determining the overall income. While agricultural income itself is exempt, it can push non-agricultural income into higher tax brackets due to this integration process. Consult your CA for further understanding of the same.

CASH TRANSACTIONS[28]

You must be very careful in entering into any cash transactions as the same may have implications for your tax outgo. Here is a pocket guide about cash transactions:

1. You are not permitted to accept ₹20,000 or more in cash

   a) For any loan or deposit, or

   b) For any amount in relation to the transfer of any immovable property (even if the transfer does not take place).

   In case of violation, a penalty of an amount equal to the amount taken in cash may be levied.

2. You cannot repay any loan, deposit, or specified advance together with interest, if any, of ₹20,000 or more.

   In case of violation, a penalty of an amount equal to the amount taken in cash may be levied.

3. No person is allowed to receive ₹2,00,000 or more in cash.

   a) In aggregate, from a person in a day; or

   b) In respect of a single transaction; or

   c) In respect of transactions relating to one event or occasion from any person.

In case of violation, a penalty u/s 271DA is levied for a sum equal to the amount of such receipt.

There are a few exceptions to the above three provisions, for example, sums received from the government, banks, a government-owned company, etc.

4. In case a person incurs any expenditure for their business or profession in respect of which payment or aggregate of payments made in cash in a day exceeds ₹10,000, then 100% of such payment will be disallowed while computing their taxable income from business or profession (refer to Section 40A (3)).

   However, some exceptions are provided (see Rule 6DD of the Income Tax Rules).

5. In case an allowance has been made with respect to any liability incurred by a person for any expenditure, and during any subsequent year, the person makes payment in respect thereof in cash, the payment is chargeable to income tax as income of the subsequent year if the payment or aggregate of payments made to a person in a day exceeds ₹10,000.

   In case payment is being made for plying, hiring, or leasing goods carriages, then the limit is ₹35,000 instead of ₹10,000.

6. In case a person incurs any expenditure for the acquisition of any asset in respect of which a payment or aggregate of payments made to a person in cash in a day exceeds ₹10,000, such an expenditure is not included in the actual cost of such an asset, and also no depreciation benefit will be available.

7. Donations made in cash to a registered trust or political party, if exceeds ₹2,000, are not allowable as a deduction under Section 80G.

8. Any payment made in cash on account of premiums on health insurance policies is not allowable as a deduction under Section 80D of the Income Tax Act.

9. Overview of Section 269SS, 269ST, 269SU, and 269T:

SECTION	COVERED TRANSACTION	THRESHOLD LIMIT	CONSEQUENCES OF DEFAULT
269SS	Taking or accepting any loan or deposit or specified sum.	₹20,000 or more	Penalty under Section 271D (100% of loan or deposit so taken or accepted).
269ST	Receipt of any amount.	₹2 lakhs or more	Penalty under Section 271DA (100% of the amount so received).
269SU	Facility to be provided for accepting payment through prescribed electronic modes.	Total sales / turnover / gross receipts exceed ₹50 crores during the immediately preceding previous year.	Penalty under Section 271DB (₹5,000 per day, during which the default continues).
269T	Repayment of any loan or deposit or specified advance.	₹20,000 or more	Penalty under Section 271E (100% of loan or deposit so repaid).

Please note, tax planning is a complicated and vast subject. It's always better to take advice from a chartered accountant or financial consultant in order to keep your taxes in check.

CHAPTER 14

ESTATE PLANNING[29]

"We don't live forever; our legacy does."
—Greg Plitt, American model and actor

Estate planning guarantees that all of your physical, intangible, financial, and online assets are distributed to the person or persons you choose after your death. Proper estate planning ensures that your assets do not wind up in legal battles for years. Legal actions unnecessarily burden your legal heirs, siblings, and family members. Effective estate planning should be your top priority to ensure the smooth succession and distribution of your estate. Generally, there are three methods of transferring assets to the successors:

1. By creating a will

2. By nomination

3. By forming a private trust

ALL ABOUT WILLS

An individual's will is a legally binding document that specifies how their estate should be distributed upon death. A person can take steps to ensure that their preferences regarding assets and properties are carried out after their death by creating a will or a trust. When a person passes away intestate (without making a will), it can cause several complications. Some people write their will by themselves or get it drafted by well-meaning friends, family members, or professionals.

The heart of the matter is that legal heirs and successors often face difficulties if there is no valid will or if the will or a portion thereof is invalid. A person's property devolves in two ways after their death:

1. According to the applicable law of succession, when a person dies intestate (i.e., the person passes away without making a will).

2. In accordance with a will (i.e., testamentary).

WHAT EXACTLY IS A WILL?

A will is a legal statement that a person (also called as a testator) makes during their lifetime regarding the disposition of their property after their death. The will does not take effect on its execution date. It begins with the date of the testator's demise. During the testator's lifetime, the will is an ambulatory document that is revocable at any time and has no legal consequence.

Wills possess two fundamental characteristics:

i) It must be intended to take effect upon the testator's demise, and it must be in writing. Just to be clear, a gift to be implemented during the donor's lifetime is a deed of settlement and not a will.

ii) It must be revocable at any time by the testator, before their death. Although wills are typically used to dispose of property, they can also be used to name executors, establish trusts, and name testamentary guardians for minor children. According to Section 63 of the Indian Succession Act of 1925, any person who has the mental capacity to make a will may revoke or amend that will at any moment.

WHO IS CAPABLE OF MAKING A WILL?

Under Section 59 of the Indian Succession Act, every adult of sound mind who is not a minor is permitted to dispose of his property via a will.

Explanation 1. A married woman may dispose of any property she could during her lifetime through her will.

Explanation 2. Persons who are differently-abled (suffering from hearing, visual, or speech impairment) and are able to create a will and are well aware of what they are doing.

Explanation 3. A person who is normally deranged may execute a will during a period of sobriety.

Explanation 4. A person should not make a will if they lack the mental clarity and knowledge to understand their actions, whether due to intoxication, illness, or any other reason.

Following are some illustrations:

i)   'A' is aware of what is happening in his immediate vicinity and is able to respond to familiar questions, but he lacks an adequate comprehension of the nature of his property, the people who are related to him, or those in whose favour he should make his will. 'A' cannot make a valid will.

ii) 'A' executes a document purporting to be his last will and testament, but he does not comprehend the nature of the document or the implications of its provisions. This document is not legitimate as a will.

iii) 'A' creates a will despite being extremely frail and incapacitated because he is able to exercise sound judgement regarding the best way to dispose of his property. This will is legitimate.

The following people are ineligible to create a will:

1. A person whose mental state is such that they have no notion of what they are doing as a result of alcohol, illness, or any other cause, including mental illness.

2. Those under 18 years of age, or minors. A minor does not attain maturity until the age of 21 if a guardian is appointed for them.

3. By their very nature, corporations are incapable of creating a will, though they may benefit from the will of an individual.

WHAT PURPOSE DOES A WILL SERVE?

In the absence of a will, an individual's property will be distributed to their legal successors in accordance with the inheritance laws applicable to them. However, the majority of individuals prefer to dispose of their properties in accordance with their own desires. Thus, it becomes necessary to create a will. In addition to this, there are following distinct advantages to drafting a will:

1. When someone dies without a will, there is often confusion among family members and relatives as to whether the deceased made a will prior to their death. However, if a will is present, the only query that must be answered is whether or not this is the last will of the testator.

2. A will is unquestionably a private document. It is primarily an expression of testator's relationship with family members, relatives, friends, and so on. A will permits the devolution of property in a personalized manner, as opposed to allowing the impersonal inheritance rules to take effect.

3. By means of a will, a parent can name a testamentary guardian for their minor offspring. A testamentary guardian is a guardian designated in a will or other testamentary document. This requires further explanation. After the demise of a parent, the law often recognizes the remaining natural parent's right to act as guardian.

4. Nonetheless, if there is no surviving parent, the law gives considerable weight to the parents' will when determining the guardian. Before appointing the proposed guardian as testamentary guardian, this issue must be discussed in depth with the proposed guardian as it is of great significance to the children's future.

5. A will addresses the specific demands and requirements of family members. For example, a father may have two sons. One

is robust, while the other has been disabled by a chronic illness since childhood. Both of these offspring would be treated equally under the inheritance laws. With a will, however, one can provide somewhat more for a disabled son, a bereaved daughter, or an ailing parent.

6. On the other hand, without a will, even the most undesirable son—who may have left the home due to disobedience, dispute, deceit, violence, etc.,—stands a chance to inherit and may return to claim his share of the father's estate. Similarly, a wife who has committed adultery may demand her inheritance according to inheritance laws.

In the absence of a will, property would be distributed in accordance with inheritance laws. The Hindu Succession Act of 1956 codifies the laws of inheritance for Buddhists, Hindus, Jains, and Sikhs. The Indian Succession Act of 1925 applies to Christians. The Parsis have a distinct inheritance law governed under the same framework as Christians. Muslims also have their own legal system (Sharia). This, however, has not been codified in law and is instead based on their religious texts. There are two main Muslim sects: Shias and Sunnis. Both have distinct inheritance regulations.

It is unfortunate that the majority of people do not have a will. Even a visionary and billionaire businessman like Dhirubhai Ambani did not leave a will.

To ensure that the wealth created by you is transferred as per your desire, you must make a will.

HOW TO PREPARE A WILL?

1. **There must be a written will**

   A will must be in writing. Military personnel on active duty for an expedition or in a war zone are the only people who are exempted from a written will. They can make a will verbally if they like. The term "privileged will" is used to describe this type of last will and testament.

2. **Muslims can make an oral will**

   Under the sharia law, a Muslim is permitted to make an oral will.

3. **No specific form**

   No specific form of will is required by law. The language employed should be straightforward, feasible and devoid of technical jargon.

4. **It need not be on a stamp paper**

   It is incorrect to state that a will must be executed on stamp paper, as the Indian Stamp Act makes no such requirement. Therefore, a will can be written on any basic sheet of paper, which must be of durable quality.

5. **Typing is not required but desired**

   A will does not require typing. It can be written by hand using any pen. A handwritten will is referred to as a holograph and is legally valid. In a handwritten will, however, the testator's illegible handwriting is destined to cause some confusion. Therefore, it is recommended that the will be typed precisely with margins on both sides of the pages.

6. Cautiousness

a) Prepare a list of your remaining assets and properties after deducting all obligations, liabilities, and expenses when drafting a will. This will help you gain a clear understanding of how you intend to distribute the estate.

b) It should be written in the language best understood by the testator in order to create the appearance that the contents were completely comprehended by the testator's desires and intentions.

c) If the testator is illiterate, the will must be carried out in a language they can understand.

d) Unusual characters should be clarified and explained in the principal body of the will. In cases where a testator disinherits and excludes his wife and other family members from the will, or leaves their entire estate to charity, it is preferable for the reasons for the bequest to be stated explicitly in the will.

WHAT LEGAL REQUIREMENTS MUST A WILL COMPLY WITH?

In accordance with Section 63 of the Indian Succession Act of 1925, "Every testator who is not a soldier engaged in an expedition or actual warfare, an airman similarly employed or engaged, or a mariner at sea, shall execute his will in accordance with the following rules:"

a) The will must be signed or authenticated in the testator's presence or by another person at his direction.

b) It is important that the testator's or his representative's signature be placed in a way that makes it obvious that this document is a will.

c) A valid will must have two individuals as witnesses apart from the one who makes the will.

WHO MAY SERVE AS A WITNESS OR EXECUTOR?

In most cases, the testator will name an executor in their will or a codicil:

- To manage the estate and ensure that the terms of the will are carried out.

- If the need for verification of the execution of the will arises later, careless witness selection could be problematic. It should be noted that the attesting witness could eventually be called to testify in court to show that the will was executed as intended.

WHAT IS A CODICIL AND HOW DO YOU CHANGE THE EXECUTOR'S NAME?

Any document relating to a will that clarifies, amends, or supplements its bequests is considered to be a part of that will. If the testator just wants to update the names of the executors by adding a few new names, a codicil may be all that is required and does not require revisions to the will's main text. A codicil can be used when the testator wants to make changes to specific bequests, such as adding or removing legatees, or when the names of beneficiaries or executors need to be changed because they have passed away. The codicil needs to be put in writing. The testator's signature and the signatures of at least two witnesses are required.

WHAT ARE THE NECESSARY DOCUMENTS AND PROCEDURES FOR MAKING A WILL?

Wills can take any form the testator deems fit; there is no standard format. It must be duly signed and witnessed before it can take effect. The will must have the testator's initials at the bottom of each page and next to any changes or additions. It is recommended that each page be fully signed. There is no need to pay stamp duty while writing or registering a will or a codicil. Writing a will on a regular paper is fine, too.

ATTESTATION

Two witnesses must be present when the testator executes the will. The testator and witnesses must sign together. However, under Hindu Law, a witness can also be a legatee (beneficiary). Parsi and Christian laws prohibit witnesses from being executors or legatees. On the other hand, if a Muslim's will is in writing, it is not obligatory for the will to be attested.

REGISTRATION

Registration of a will is optional under Section 18 of the Registration Act. However, it is substantial legal evidence that the correct parties stood before the registering officers, and the will was later attested after verifying their identities. The Registrar or Sub-registrar registers wills for a nominal charge. The testator and witnesses must attend the registrar's office.

Registration allows the Registrar or Sub-registrar to provide a certified duplicate of the will if it is lost or destroyed. If the will is contested, registration enhances its credibility.

WHEN MUST A WILL BE EXECUTED?

The executor of the will or a testator's heir may petition for probate after the testator's demise. The court will inquire if any of the deceased's other heirs have objections to the will. Probate is granted automatically if no objections are filed with the court.

A probate is a court-certified copy of a will and should be considered conclusive proof that a will is genuine.

In the event that any heirs raise objections, a citation must be served requesting their consent. This must be conspicuously displayed in the courtroom. If there are no further objections, the probate will be granted and only then does the will take effect.

NOMINATION

WHAT EXACTLY IS NOMINATION?

The act of nominating is referred to as a nomination. It is a process wherein a person is appointed as the beneficiary and is entitled to receive the proceeds of the investment or assets on the demise of the investor. For example, investments or assets in LIC or GIC, banks, mutual funds, co-operative societies, and so on.

WHO CAN NOMINATE?

Nomination can be done only by an investor or policyholder who is a major and holds accounts, investment certificates, insurance policies, bonds, demat accounts, fixed deposits, etc., and the nomination facility is only open to those acting individually or collectively.

WHEN CAN THE NOMINATION BE DONE?

Nomination is typically done at the time of investment or account opening by filing a relevant nomination form.

IS CHANGING THE NOMINATION ALLOWED AT ANY TIME? IF SO, HOW MANY TIMES?

Yes, the old nomination can be removed, and a new nomination can be submitted without informing the previous nominee.

TO WHOM ARE THE NOMINATION FACILITIES PROVIDED?

Nomination is available to individuals who are majors (minors cannot nominate).

1. A HUF, firm, companies, etc., can't nominate.
2. A nominee can't nominate another nominee.
3. Those holding assets in a representative capacity (like trustees, liquidators, treasurers, bank managers, etc.) cannot nominate.

WHO CAN BE APPOINTED AS A NOMINEE?

A nominee could be an adult or a child depending on their age. If a person under the age of majority (18 years old) is selected to serve as a nominee, a legal guardian must be appointed to serve in that capacity until the minor reaches the age of majority.

WHAT ARE THE RIGHTS OF A NOMINEE?

A nominee has the right to receive the invested amount, securities, insured amount, etc., in the event of the death of the original investor, but they do not become the owner of the same. The ownership will depend upon the testamentary will or any other arrangement of succession made by the investor or policyholder. A nominee is a mere trustee of the investor or the security holder.

It is best to have the same person serve as both the nominee and the beneficiary of the will to avoid any potential disagreements in the future.

As far as financial assets are concerned, nomination plays an important role in the following assets:

- Bank accounts
- Fixed deposits
- Bank lockers
- Demat accounts

If the formality of nomination has been complied with, the transmission is done in the following manner:

A.	Death of a single holder	In favour of the nominee
B.	Death of one of the joint holders	In favour of surviving joint holder
C.	Death of all the joint holders	In favour of the nominee

If there is no nomination, then transmission is in favour of the legal heirs. However, if one of the joint holders dies, then transmission is done in favour of the surviving joint holder.

The above rule applies to fixed deposits and lockers as well. However, in the case of a locker, before handing over the articles to the nominee, the bank must comply with certain formalities.

DEMAT ACCOUNTS

In demat accounts, not only can you specify up to three nominees but you can also specify the percentage of share of each nominee.

The presumption of equal distribution among the nominees applies if no percentage has been set.

The rules that apply in case of nomination in banks also apply to demat accounts. In demat accounts, it is permitted to opt out of making a nomination. However, it is always advisable to provide the names of nominees. In demat accounts, the signatures of witnesses are not required in the following cases:

- If the nomination form is signed by the account users with a wet signature.
- E-signing is used to sign an online nomination form.

However, when a thumb print is used instead of a signature, a witness signature is still required.

The situation with a joint demat account changes slightly in the event of the death of one of the account holders. The depository participant will freeze the demat account and distribute any residual monies to the beneficiaries' demat accounts upon receipt of a notarized death certificate.

MUTUAL FUNDS

When it comes to mutual fund schemes, demat account rules apply.

However, there are rules about what will happen if a nominee dies. If the nominee dies before the mutual fund investor, the nomination is cancelled immediately. If multiple people are nominated, and one of them dies before the claim is paid out, that person's share would be split evenly among the other nominees.

In the event of death of the investor, the nominees have to comply with the following:

- KYC process
- Proof of death
- Signature of the nominee, duly attested
- Proof of guardianship, in case the nominee is a minor

It is advisable to keep a copy of the nomination form with the bank, depository, or mutual funds.

PRIVATE FAMILY TRUST

A will has its own limitations. For example, it is most likely to be challenged. Also, it is not possible to maintain ownership or control of assets in a common pool in a will, which causes the family wealth to be divided. Therefore, one must explore a way of estate planning through private trusts for the benefit of family members.

A trust, according to its official definition, is a legal relationship in which the owner of an asset or right (the settlor) entrusts it to another person or entity (the trustee/s) for the benefit of another (the beneficiary).

The creation of a private trust is particularly advisable for someone who owns multiple assets and wishes to dictate the manner in which certain property should be enjoyed by the beneficiaries, or to create a long-lasting mechanism for the operation of family-owned businesses.

Speculation about the introduction of an estate duty by the government has also spurred many business families to consider creating private trusts to safeguard their wealth.

Whilst gifts made during the lifetime of a person is a simple process, it technically means that the person loses control over the assets. Therefore, one must opt for a gift only if the decision to gift the assets is irreversible.

Any sum of money or property received under a will or as a gift is exempt from any taxes, but charges such as stamp duty, registration fees, and municipal taxes will still be levied. In case of gifts (Section 56), the Income Tax Act must be looked into, if a person receives an immovable property without paying anything from any person other than relatives and the stamp duty value of that property exceeds ₹50,000, then such stamp duty value shall be taxable in their hands. The difference between the stamp duty value and the amount paid for a piece of property from someone who is not a relative of yours and that you receive as payment is taxable if it exceeds ₹50,000. Furthermore, when property is settled under a trust, it is exempt from taxation.

It is important to note that setting up a trust is more complicated than making a will. You must hire a solicitor or an experienced lawyer or a specialist advisor to plan your estate through private trusts.

"Estate planning is an important and everlasting gift you can give your family. And setting up a smooth inheritance isn't as hard as you might think."
—Suze Orman, American financial advisor and author

CHAPTER 15

WHAT EVERY FAMILY MUST KNOW

"Record management is knowing what you have, where you have it and how long you have to keep it."
—Anonymous

You have worked hard throughout your life. You have a number of assets like stocks, real estate, metals, and also legal rights in the country you're living. While these assets have a long shelf life, you will not. So, you must meticulously maintain your records to ensure smooth succession. Succession planning is often neglected by most of us, leading to insurmountable difficulties for legal heirs in compiling an inventory of all your assets. Not only must your heirs be aware of your assets but they must also be informed about your liabilities and other pertinent information. This chapter will help you organize your state of affairs systematically to ensure effortless succession after you are gone.

If you are involved in a business or profession, you should have a plan for its continuity through proper succession planning. Often, disputes arise after the person's death among their heirs regarding the entitlement of their estate. Proper documentation can help avoid conflicts and litigation.

It is equally important for your successor to preserve your values, beliefs, culture, and traditions. For instance, if you have established a charitable trust that provides yeoman service to society, wouldn't you want to continue beyond your lifetime, passing on from generation to generation? Often, such an organization faces challenges after the demise of the successor or trustees.

The whole idea is to keep the entire information readily available so that your successor does not run helter-skelter when you are no longer there to assist. Maintaining important details of your finances and legal information is a must so that your successors do not face any inconvenience when you are no longer present.

The following information should be recorded in a notebook or a journal, or Excel sheet:

1. BASIC INFORMATION

- PAN card details of all family members, business partners, key staff, and ex-employers.
- Aadhaar card number, passport details, driving license, credit cards, debit cards, membership cards of club and associations, ration card, voter card, mobile and landline phone numbers, complete details of safe deposit lockers, etc.

2. BANK ACCOUNTS

Details of bank accounts, including the name and address of the branch, name of nominees, and details of joint holders etc. Details of pension accounts, if any, should also be recorded.

3. DEPOSITS AND INVESTMENTS

Full details of all fixed deposits, recurring deposits, bonds, stocks, demat accounts, debentures, provident funds, mutual funds, etc., should be documented appropriately.

4. PROFESSIONALS, SUPPLIERS, AND SERVICE PROVIDERS

Contact details of all professionals you have hired, along with the nature of services they render must be documented. Specify clearly if any original documents are with them.

5. PRESENCE ON THE INTERNET AND SOCIAL MEDIA

Record your digital presence on social media platforms like Facebook, LinkedIn, YouTube, Instagram, Google, and X (formerly Twitter), e-mail account, etc., along with usernames and passwords.

6. VEHICLES

Details of vehicles you own, along with details of any loans availed against them. Vehicles include cars, scooters, motorcycle, trucks, tempos, boats, etc.

7. TAXATION AND STATUTORY INFORMATION

This includes information related to income tax, profession tax, Employees State Insurance Corporation (ESIC), provident fund, GST, Director Identification Number (DIN), etc.

8. INSURANCE

Ensure that complete details of life insurance, health insurance, vehicle insurance, indemnity insurance, fire or theft insurance policies are maintained properly.

9. IMMOVABLE PROPERTIES

Details of immovable properties, including their location, area, and registration should be properly maintained.

10. MOVABLE PROPERTIES

This includes precious metals, debtors, receivables, etc.

11. BORROWINGS, GUARANTEES, AND OTHER LIABILITIES

Full details of all secured and unsecured loans and guarantee given.

12. WILL AND POWER OF ATTORNEY

Will, codicils, and powers of attorney are important documents and must be retrievable by your family members.

13. DOCUMENTS

Some records are temporary, however, there are many documents of permanent nature which are helpful not only during a lifetime but even after death. I always advise my clients to maintain a master file of all important documents. This will ensure that they are retrievable when required.

At the top of the document, keep an index of all documents with serial and page numbers. If the original documents are in the master file, you may paginate with a pencil. The master file should be a durable box file. You may have more than one master file if necessary. Keep the master file safe at your residence (not in your office). A photocopy or soft copy should also be maintained as a backup.

I suggest you get my other book—*What Every Family Must Know: Ultimate Workbook for Smooth Succession and Estate Planning*. This workbook is ideal for recording all your information for smooth succession planning.

CHAPTER 16

MANAGE YOUR RISK

"We must give more in order to get more. It is the generous giving of ourselves that produces the generous harvest."
—Orison Swett Marden, American author

RISK MANAGEMENT

Uncertainty surrounds us in every area of life —be it health, career, or the environment. Where there is uncertainty, there is a risk of mishaps, breakdowns, loss, or injury. It is our bounden duty to identify these risks and take steps to mitigate them. While we cannot avoid most of these risks, we can plan to circumvent those that are avoidable. Sound financial planning may help you reduce the loss of wealth to a tolerable level.

Another way to manage risk is to transfer it to a risk-taker, such as an insurer charging us a premium to take the risk on our behalf. Insurance is a legally binding agreement between an insurer and the insured individual or entity. Protecting your assets from unforeseen circumstances is essential, and an insurance policy is one of the best ways to achieve this. You can protect yourself against accidents, health hazards, critical illnesses, legal liabilities, professional liabilities, theft, fire, death, etc. Let us discuss health insurance and life insurance in more detail.

HEALTH INSURANCE

Health insurance covers your medical expenses related to hospitalization due to illness. It may include ancillary expenses such as medicines, physiotherapy, doctor's fees, pre- and post-hospitalization expenses, etc. Some policies cover specific illnesses like cancer. The real challenge one may face is choosing the correct policy from among the hundreds available in the market. There is a definite advantage to seeking help of an insurance advisor. However, I have outlined a few pointers that must be considered while purchasing health insurance:

1. Health insurance may be purchased online or offline. Buy it from a reputable insurance advisor who can help you when needed—for example, in filing a claim, settling a claim, and preparing documents properly so that the claim is accepted. However, you can buy it online if you have the time and knowledge to complete the formalities, as it is often cheaper.

2. Ensure that the name and birth date in the policy match exactly with those to your Aadhaar and PAN cards.

3. Disclose all the relevant information about your health, medical history, and habits or addictions, such as smoking.

4. Pay the premium before due date and renew your policy when it is due. Even if you face financial difficulties, you must prioritize paying the premium, as health issues can arise at any time without warning.

5. Purchase a policy as early as possible in your life. The younger you are, the lower the premium, and the broader the coverage. This also ensures that the waiting period for specific diseases is duly served.

6. If you are employed, you might enjoy the employer's group health plan. However, it is still wise to have an independent policy to ensure continuous protection.

7. Inflation is always a major concern, especially in the case of medical treatments and education. In metro cities, medical costs have skyrocketed, so choose a policy that optimally serves your purpose and needs, and also protects you without depleting your savings. If you live in a smaller town, a policy of ₹5 lakhs to ₹10 lakhs may be sufficient. However, in large metros, this amount should be at least double. Remember to cover all your family members with a floater policy.

8. Check the claims settlement ratio of the insurance company on its website. The Insurance Regulatory and Development Authority of India (IRDAI) occasionally makes this data public.

9. Examine the co-pay and sub-limit clauses carefully. In co-pay arrangements, the insured bears part of the expenses. Sub-limit refers to the maximum amount payable by the insurance company for certain expenses, such as room rent in hospitals.

10. Once you have a basic policy, consider a top-up plan. The premium of a top plan is significantly lower than that of a regular plan.

11. Compare the policy you intend to buy with others available in the market. However, always remember that a cheap policy may not always be the best. Consider other parameters, such

as claim settlement ratio, sub-limits, waiting period, pre-existing disease clauses, etc.

12. Be mindful of the no-claim bonus clause.

13. If possible, have a separate critical illness plan and accident cover for additional protection.

14. Purchase health insurance early in life. If you are employed, buy it in your 40s. Elderly individuals have to pay higher premiums, and, sometimes, it is challenging to take a policy; for example, an insurance company may be unwilling to cover you after a heart attack.

LIFE INSURANCE

You must protect those you love after your death. Life insurance policies have traditionally offered several benefits, such as:

- Tax deductions
- Long-term savings
- Investments that provide access to funds when needed
- Collateral security to financial institutions
- Financial protection for your family
- Peace of mind to dependents

With plenty of available options, one has to choose the best policy based on one's needs. First, it's not a good idea to mix investment with protection. Be clear whether you are buying a policy for investment purposes or to protect your family in case of the breadwinner's demise. Need-based insurance is the new normal. I make it absolutely clear that I am not against life insurance products. Even unit-linked insurance policies (ULIPS) have evolved and now offer options to the insured to invest in a mix of equities, debt, and other asset classes. However, you must weigh the benefits and return on investment for any products you buy.

How much is the coverage? In many cases, I find that both coverage and returns are abysmally low. Therefore, you must assess how much your family will need if something happens to you. Insurance is only a small part of your total portfolio. You must take a holistic view after considering two factors:

1. Your total portfolio
2. Your asset-allocation plan

Consider the percentage of your total portfolio you have provided for insurance in your asset-allocation plan. Once this is clear, the rest becomes simple. If it is 5%, then you are only partially relying on insurance to grow wealth and protect your family. You have other avenues. Yet, as a measure of risk management, insurance plays an important role. It helps the bereaved family to face liabilities of the deceased, everyday expenses, education, wedding expenses, and more.

My advice to my clients is to balance protection and investments. In most cases, term insurance combined with mutual fund investments serves the purpose.

While buying term insurance, look beyond today's expenses. What will your future expenses be say after 15 or 25 years from now? Whether the sum assured will meet these expenses when your family needs it? We have elaborately discussed how much fund is ideal in

Chapter 12, *Enjoy the Golden Years of Your Life*. You may also choose an insurance cover with a level-up feature, which allows you to increase the amount of sum assured over time.

For example, if you buy a term plan for an assured sum of ₹1 crore, the premium payable will be ₹20,000. For the same coverage in a traditional policy, the premium would be more than ₹60,000 per year. Traditional policies offer returns of around 4% to 6%, while investments may yield double that amount. After investing in the term plan, you can invest the balance amount in other avenues to derive maximum benefit. Premiums paid in a term plan are non-refundable, but this is more than compensated for by other investments. At the same time, you will follow the golden rule of not mixing insurance with investment. The sole objective of the term plan is security, so treat the premium paid as a normal day-to-day expense.

A term insurance plan may be bought as soon as you start earning. The biggest advantage is that your premium is fixed when you buy the policy and does not increase, unlike health insurance. In other words, it is inflation-proof. Though I advised you to buy health insurance through an agent, term plans may be purchased online to save money. As discussed earlier, select the life insurance company the way you would for health insurance.

Give top priority to protecting your loved ones. I always advise clients to secure their health insurance first, then create a reserve fund, take out a life insurance policy, and finally invest. Once you do this, your journey towards financial freedom will be smooth and enjoyable. Suze Orman rightly says, "Your state of mind has a direct effect on your finances. Knowing that you have cared for the people you love always frees up major blocks on this path to financial freedom. If you take this step, you will feel free already in mind, body, and soul."

WHAT IS BETTER: BUYING OR RENTING A HOUSE?

In our country, buying a house is often an emotional decision. A roof over one's head is a dream every middle-class person aspires. Owning a house becomes a matter of pride. It allows you to enjoy your life without the frequent distractions and hassles of moving. Additionally, owning a home enables intergenerational inheritance, and an ancestral house carries cultural value and cherished memories. It gives you a sense of ownership and stability during retirement.

Moreover, a house is a financial asset that can be sold if necessary. It's an appreciating asset, as real estate prices generally rise over time. If you do not use property yourself, it can always be rented out, to generate passive income.

However, if you have a large housing loan, the EMI could become a burden in case of setbacks like job loss. As discussed earlier, plan carefully before buying a house to ensure you will be able to manage the loan. One common mistake many of us make is not setting a clear goal to buy a house. You can save separately for a house over a reasonable period, say five to ten years, and then buy the house with this fund. Any shortfall can be compensated with a small, manageable housing loan. You are in the safe zone if your equated monthly installments are less than 30% of your monthly net income.

There are a few exceptions to buying a house. You might choose a rented house if your job is subject to frequent transfers to various locations. If you have not saved enough for a down payment, you may need to rent. If the house is beyond your budget, there is no point in overstressing and carrying the loan burden for 20 or 30 years.

My advice is to not be overwhelmed, underwhelmed, or swayed by the calculations that tell you why renting a house is better than buying. These are somebody else's numbers. Do not consider them as a problem-solving manual. Make your own calculations.

CREATE WEALTH, NOT LIABILITIES

In *Rich Dad, Poor Dad*, Robert T. Kiyosaki says, "Rich people acquire assets. The poor and middle-class acquire liabilities—which they think are assets. An asset puts money in your pocket. A liability takes money from your pocket."

An asset is something that holds monetary value. It may be liquid cash, bank balances, stocks, gold, silver, or real estate. Ideally, an asset will appreciate over time. On the other hand, liabilities are debts you acquire, such as home loans, credit card loans, business loans, or personal loans.

Before buying an asset, ensure that its value will increase and generate some passive income. The moment you acquire such assets; your money starts working for you. If your return on assets beats the inflation rate, your asset will grow faster. On the other hand, liabilities may grow disproportionately and lead to financial burnout in the long run. Therefore, focus on buying assets, not liabilities. This one habit will significantly enhance your journey towards financial freedom.

MISTAKES TO AVOID WHILE PLANNING RETIREMENT

- Not starting early

- Ignoring health insurance

- Overlooking inflation

- Not diversifying your portfolio

- Transferring house to kids during lifetime

- Depending too much on children

- Investing too much in real estate

- Being greedy and chasing returns

- Not making a will

- Lastly, not pursuing your passion and hobbies

"You may not control all the events that happen to you, but you can decide not to be reduced by them."

—Maya Angelou, American memoirist and poet

ENDNOTES

CHAPTER 1

1 *Life Positive* magazine, August 2023.

2 *No Limits: The Will to Succeed* by Michael Phelps with Alan Abrahamson (Simon and Schuster, UK Ltd.).

3 *Massive Action Equals Massive Results* by Sunil Saxena, M. D.

4 *The Breakthrough: 11 Trailblazers. One Movement* by Megha Bajaj.

5 *The 10X Rule* by Grant Cardone.

6 *The Breakthrough: 11 Trailblazers. One Movement* by Megha Bajaj.

CHAPTER 2

7 *The 9 steps to Financial Freedom* by Suze Orman.

8 *Secrets of the Millionaire Mind: Mastering the Inner Game of Wealth* by T. Harv Eker.

9 *Tata Stories* by Harish Bhatt.

10 *What Is Your WHY: Your Why Will Make You Succeed* by Shairdel Saleh.

11 This part is based on various articles published in *Life Positive* magazine, in October 2007, January 2017, March 2017, and January 2020.

12 *Mudras & Health Perspectives: An Indian Approach* by Suman K. Chiplunkar.

13 *Financial Freedom: A Promised Opportunity for You* by Manish Lath and Mukesh Kumar Agrawal.

14 *Angels Speak: Your Daily Dose of Divine Love* by Roshani (Shenazz Nadirshah)

CHAPTER 5

15   *The Breakthrough: 11 Trailblazers. One Movement* by Megha Bajaj.

16   *NR Narayana Murthy - A Biography* by Ritu Singh.

17   The partha system provides a single-page snapshot of profit and loss on a daily basis. Simply put, it means answering the question: "Aaj kitna pada?", or "How much did it cost to produce one unit at a plant?".

18   If you are interested in learning Li Ka-Shing's strategy in depth, I suggest you read *Li Ka-Shing and Cheung Kong Holdings: A Business and Life Biography* by Yan Qicheng. (Published by LID Publishing Limited, London.)

CHAPTER 9

19   But if you do that, the eggs will rot and you will end up only with the basket. So, don't put all your investments in one class of asset; diversify your portfolio and reduce the risk.

20   What Are Asset Classes? More Than Just Stocks and Bonds. https://www.investopedia.com/terms/a/assetclasses.asp (Investopedia.com)

21   www.investopedia.com.

CHAPTER 10

22   *Believe and Achieve W. Clement Stone's 17 Principles of Success* by Samuel A. Cypert

23   75% of Indians don't have an emergency fund, can default on EMIs in case of a sudden lay off: Survey. *The Times of India* article dated February 28, 2023.

24   India's Money Habits 2023: Survey by Finology Ventures.

25   Liquid assets are those assets that can be quickly converted into cash because they have a liquid market and are safe. When liquidated, their values remain relatively constant. For e.g., bank balances, cash, fixed deposits, recurring deposits, precious metals such as gold and silver, short-term bonds, liquid mutual fund investments.

CHAPTER 11

26 This chapter has been contributed by Harshad Chetanwala, CFP (CM), co-founder of MyWealthGrowth.com.

CHAPTER 13

27 This chapter has been contributed by CA Shashikant Maiya, a senior chartered accountant from Mumbai. You can reach him at: shashikantmaiya@gmail.com.

28 Brochure published by Directorate of Income Tax.

CHAPTER 14

29 This chapter has been contributed by CA Vimal Punmiya, a well-known senior chartered accountant from Mumbai. You can reach him at: vimalpunmiya@gmail.com.

AUTHOR'S NOTE

In the course of your journey toward financial freedom, you might encounter some stumbling blocks. Problems do not come with a manual. Each of us has to find our own path. Whatever works for you is the thing that matters the most.

My objective of writing this book is to simply help you become more resilient to failure. You fail, you learn, you unlearn, and you learn again. Change is burdensome, but it is worth it.

I hope this book resonates with you, dear readers. I would love to hear your success stories.

In the end, let me assure you that financial freedom is your birthright; it's your responsibility; and it's possible—you can do it! I wish that you soon enter an era of great accomplishment, prosperity, and joy.

With love,

Pawan Kr Agarwal

JAICO PUBLISHING HOUSE

Elevate Your Life. Transform Your World.

ESTABLISHED IN 1946, Jaico Publishing House is home to world-transforming authors such as Robin Sharma, Sadhguru, Osho, the Dalai Lama, Deepak Chopra, Eknath Easwaran, Paramhansa Yogananda, Devdutt Pattanaik, Radhakrishnan Pillai, Morgan Housel, Napoleon Hill, John Maxwell, Brian Tracy, and Stephen Hawking.

Our late founder Mr. Jaman Shah first established Jaico as a book distribution company. Sensing that independence was around the corner, he aptly named his company Jaico ('Jai' means victory in Hindi). In order to service the significant demand for affordable books in a developing nation, Mr. Shah initiated Jaico's own publications. Jaico was India's first publisher of paperback books in the English language.

While self-help; religion and philosophy; mind, body and spirit; and business titles form the cornerstone of our non-fiction list, we publish an exciting range of current affairs, history, biography, art and architecture, travel, and popular science books as well. Our renewed focus on popular fiction is evident in our new titles by a host of fresh young talent from India and abroad.

Jaico's translations division publishes select bestselling titles in over 10 regional languages including Gujarati, Hindi, Kannada, Malayalam, Marathi, Tamil, and Telugu. These include titles from renowned national and international authors like Sudha Murthy, Gaur Gopal Das, Swami Mukundananda, Jay Shetty, Simon Sinek, Ankur Warikoo and Jeff Keller.

Boasting one of India's largest book distribution networks, Jaico has its headquarters in Mumbai, with branches in Ahmedabad, Bangalore, Chennai, Delhi, Hyderabad, and Kolkata. This network ensures that our books reach all parts of the country, both urban and rural.

Visit our Website

www.ingramcontent.com/pod-product-compliance
Lightning Source LLC
Chambersburg PA
CBHW071536200326
41519CB00021BB/6510